The Observers Series
AIRLINERS

About the Book

Observers Airliners provides an invaluable pocket guide to the major types of aircraft used regularly by the world's airlines. Ninety different airliners are described and illustrated (with photographs and silhouettes throughout), ranging from the newest products of such giants as Boeing, British Aerospace and Airbus to the elderly but still useful classics such as the DC-3 and the Viscount. Here, too, will be found details of types yet to enter service when the book was published, among them the Boeing 777 and a new generation of Soviet airliners being prepared for introduction in the nineties. Important smaller types are included, too, although these have been restricted to those used for regularly-scheduled services, with a minimum of 19 passenger seats. Data have been corrected to the beginning of 1991.

About the Authors

William Green, compiler of *Observers Aircraft* for 39 years, is internationally known for many works of aviation reference. William Green entered aviation journalism during the early years of World War II, subsequently served with the RAF and resumed aviation writing in 1947. Until the end of 1990 he was managing editor of one of the largest circulation European-based aviation journals, *Air International*, and co-editor of *Air Enthusiast*.

Gordon Swanborough has spent virtually the whole of his working life as an aviation journalist and author, since joining Temple Press in 1943 on the staff of *The Aeroplane Spotter*. He recently retired after some 20 years as editor of *Air International* and co-editor, with William Green, of *Air Enthusiast*.

The *Observer's* series was launched in 1937 with the publication of *The Observer's Book of Birds*. Today, over fifty years later, paperback *Observers* continue to offer practical useful information on a wide range of subjects, and with every book regularly revised by experts, the facts are right up-to-date. Students, amateur enthusiasts and professional organizations alike will find the latest *Observers* invaluable.

'Thick and glossy, briskly informative' – *The Guardian*

'If you are a serious spotter of any of the things the series deals with, the books must be indispensable' – *The Times Educational Supplement*

AIRLINERS

William Green and Gordon Swanborough

with silhouettes by Dennis Punnett

FREDERICK WARNE

FREDERICK WARNE
Published by the Penguin Group
27 Wrights Lane, London W8 5TZ, England
Penguin Books USA Inc., 375 Hudson Street, New York, New York 10014, USA
Penguin Books Australia Ltd, Ringwood, Victoria, Australia
Penguin Books Canada Ltd, 2801 John Street, Markham, Ontario, Canada L3R 1B4
Penguin Books (NZ) Ltd, 182–190 Wairau Road, Auckland 10, New Zealand

Penguin Books Ltd, Registered Offices: Harmondsworth, Middlesex, England

First published 1983
Third edition 1991

ISBN 0 7232 3567 8

Typeset, printed and bound in Great Britain by
William Clowes Limited, Beccles and London

INTRODUCTION

AS this third edition of *Observers Airliners* goes to press early in 1991, the world's airline business is again passing through a period of stress—a situation not entirely without precedent. After a poor start to the 'eighties, the airlines had enjoyed a period of rapid growth in the second half of the decade. With business and leisure travellers flying in ever-increasing numbers and a degree of stability returning to the industry after the upheaval caused by deregulation in the USA, the airlines were able to set about replenishing their fleets, and the order books of the manufacturers grew accordingly. By the end of 1989, most of the leading builders of commercial aircraft—notably Airbus, Boeing, Fokker and McDonnell Douglas—had backlogs equal to or better than at any time previously.

The events of 1990 brought the first indication of another downturn in the airlines' fortunes, however. Moves towards liberalization of air transport (deregulation within limits) in Europe, the consequences of the democratization of East European nations and the unification of Germany all helped to change the status and prospects for many airlines, threatening the continued existence of some and offering others unexpected scope for expansion. Threats of recession, in the New World and the Old, suggested that traffic growth would slow down, whilst the crisis in the Gulf following Iraq's illegal occupation of Kuwait sent fuel prices soaring and passenger numbers slumping.

Writing in the second edition of this title, four years ago, the authors suggested that the advent of the propfan as a prime mover for future airliners was imminent. This proved not to be the case, since fuel costs remained stable and low—thus depriving the propfan of one of its major selling points vis-à-vis today's highly efficient turbofans. If the cost of aviation fuel remained at the inflated levels of late 1990, however, it seemed likely that the propfan might again be considered as the power plant for the next generation of airliners. Meanwhile, the airlines have a broad range of turbofan and turboprop types from which to choose, as the content of this volume reveals.

We have chosen, for this edition, to exclude some of the smaller types of aircraft previously included, retaining only those with a normal passenger capacity of 19 seats or more. Also, those aircraft types exclusively or primarily used only for freight carrying have been covered in a slightly condensed form, grouped at the end of the book.

These changes have made it possible to include separate entries for the growing number of variants of several important types, as well as those new types that have been launched since 1987. In this latter category there are nine new aircraft, including the first two of the new breed of regional jets; four twin-turboprop types for the commuter industry, and, at the top end in size and range, the Airbus A330 and A340 and the Boeing 777. Variants making a first appearance in this edition are the Airbus A321, Boeing 737-400, BAe Jetstream 41 and McDonnell Douglas MD-90.

Other new types are on the horizon and some of these probably will be launched in the lifetime of this volume. On both sides of the Atlantic, interest is being shown especially in regional jets in the 80/130-seat bracket, with Deutsche Aerospace, Aérospatiale, Alenia, CASA, British Aerospace and Fokker numbered among the companies discussing the possibilities of collaborating to launch aircraft in this category. Indonesia's IPTN hopes to launch a 50-seat twin-turboprop, there are numerous projects under study in the Soviet Union as the design bureaux there seek to diversify from military activities, and, in a longer timescale, the European and US industries are looking toward a new supersonic transport to follow Concorde.

In view of the uncertainties to which we have already alluded, it is impossible to put a time-scale upon these potential developments. Perhaps the *fourth* edition of *Observers Airliners* will provide some of the answers. Meanwhile it is hoped that this edition will provide readers with the 'facts-at-your-fingertips' reference source for which the Observers Series is renowned.

FGS/WG

AUTHORS' ACKNOWLEDGEMENT

The authors wish to thank the public relations staffs of the principal manufacturers whose products are represented in this book, for assistance with data and photographs. Grateful acknowledgement is also made to the following for their assistance with photographs: John A. Bradley, Austin Brown, G. Jennings, Geoffrey P. Jones, Brian Pickering/Military Aircraft Photographs, John W. R. Taylor and Lech Zielaskowski.

AEROSPATIALE CARAVELLE

Country of Origin: France
Type: Short-to-medium-range jet transport.
Power Plant (Caravelle 10B): Two 14,500 lb st (64,4 kN) Pratt & Whitney JT8D-9 turbofans.
Performance (Caravelle 10B): Max cruising speed, 445 kts (825 km/h) at 25,000 ft (7 620 m); range with max payload, 1,450 naut mls (2 650 km); range with max fuel, 1,965 naut mls (3 640 km).
Accommodation: Flight crew of three and up to 110 passengers five-abreast with one aisle at 29-in (74-cm) pitch; typical mixed-class layout for 91.
Status: Prototypes first flown on 25 May 1955 and 6 May 1956; certification 2 April 1958; first production Caravelle I flown 18 May 1958 and first service (Air France) flown on 6 May 1959. First flights of later variants: Caravelle IA, 11 February 1960; III, 30 December 1959; VI-N, 10 September 1960; VI-R, 6 February 1961; VII, 29 December 1960; 10A, 31 August 1962; 10B/Super B, 3 March 1964; 10R, 18 January 1965; 11R, 21 April 1967; 12, 29 October 1970. Production ended 1972.
Sales: Production total 282, including three prototypes; 20 Caravelle I; 12 IA; 78 III; 53 VI-N; 56 VI-R; one VII; one 10A; 22 10B; 20 10R; six 11R; 12 Super Caravelle 12.
Notes: Caravelle Mks I, IA, III and VI had same overall dimensions, different engine versions and weights. Caravelle Mks VII, 10, 11 and 12 featured JT8D engines in place of original Rolls-Royce Avons, and the Caravelle 11 and 12 introduced fuselage stretches of 3 ft 0½ in (0.93 m) and 10 ft 7 in (3.21 m) respectively. About 65 Caravelles of assorted type were in airline service in 1991, particularly with charter airlines in Europe. *Photo:* Caravelle VI-N.

AEROSPATIALE CARAVELLE 10B

Dimensions (Caravelle 10B): Span, 112 ft 6 in (34,30 m); length, 108 ft 3½ in (33,01 m); height, 28 ft 7 in (8,72 m); wing area, 1,579 sq ft (146,7 m²).
Weights (Caravelle 10B): Operating weight empty, 66,260 lb (30 055 kg); max payload, 20,060 lb (9 100 kg); max take-off, 123,460 lb (56 000 kg); max landing, 109,130 lb (49 500 kg).

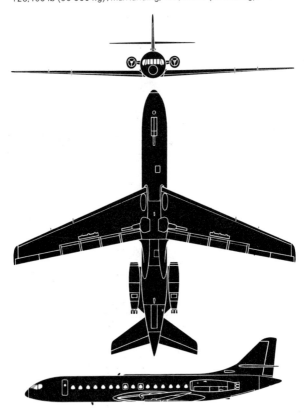

AEROSPATIALE (NORD) 262 FREGATE

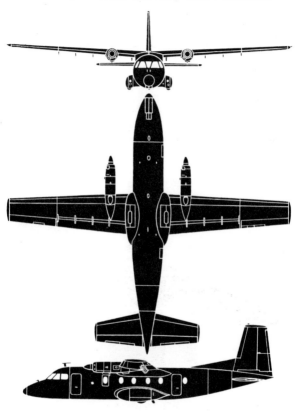

Dimensions: Span, 74 ft 2 in (22,60 m); length, 63 ft 3 in (19,28 m); height, 20 ft 4 in (6,21 m); wing area, 592 sq ft (55,0 m²).
Weights: Basic operating, 15,929 lb (7 225 kg); max payload, 6,781 lb (3 075 kg); max zero fuel, 22,710 lb (10 300 kg); max take-off, 23,810 lb (10 800 kg); max landing, 23,040 lb (10 450 kg).

AEROSPATIALE (NORD) 262C

Country of Origin: France.

Type: Short-range turboprop transport.

Power Plant (N262C): Two 1,130 shp (843 kW) Turboméca Bastan VIIC turboprops.

Performance (N262C): Max cruise, 225 kts (415 km/h) at 20,000 ft (6 100 m); range with max payload (26 passengers), 565 mls (915 km); range with max fuel, 985 naut mls (1 825 km).

Accommodation: Flight crew of two and up to 29 passengers, three-abreast with offset aisle at 33-in (84-cm) seat pitch.

Status: MH-250 prototype flown 20 May 1959; MH-260 prototype flown 29 July 1960; Nord 262 prototype flown 24 December 1962, certificated 16 July 1964. First production (262B) flown 8 July 1964, first 262A flown early 1965, certificated March, entered service August. N262C flown July 1968 and certificated 24 December 1970. Mohawk 298 conversion flown 7 January 1975, certificated 19 October 1976. Production completed 1975.

Sales: Production total 110, including four N262B, 67 N262A and military orders for N262D Frégate.

Notes: The Nord 262 design was based on the original unpressurized Super Broussard project of the Max Holste company, which built one piston-engined MH-250 and a prototype plus 10 pre-production MH-260s with Bastan turboprops. Nord developed a pressurized circular-section fuselage for the N262, built in four variants, during which time the company merged with Sud to form Aérospatiale. In the USA, nine N262s were converted to Mohawk 298 standard with PT6A-45 engines and systems improvements, deriving this designation from FAR Part 298 airworthiness requirements. About 25 Nord 262s/Mohawk 298s were in airline service at the end of 1990.

AEROSPATIALE/ALENIA ATR 42

Country of Origin: France and Italy.
Type: Short-range regional airliner.
Power Plant: Two flat-rated 1,800 shp (1 342 kW) Pratt & Whitney PW120 or 1,950 shp (1 454 kW) PW121 turboprops.
Performance (ATR 42-200): Max cruising speed, 268 kts (497 km/h) at 17,000 ft (5 180 m); range with max payload, 1,050 naut mls (1 946 km); range with max fuel, 2,420 naut mls (4 481 km).
Accommodation: Flight crew of two and up to 50 passengers four-abreast with single aisle at 30-in (76-cm) pitch; typical layout for 42 passengers.
Status: Two prototype/development aircraft, first flown 16 August and 31 October 1984. First production aircraft flown 30 April 1985. French certification of ATR 42–200 and ATR 42–300 on 24 September 1985, and first services flown by Air Littoral on 9 December. FAA certification on 25 October 1985 followed by deliveries to first US customer, Command Airways.
Sales: Total of 283 firm sales and 49 options. 185 delivered by January 1991.
Notes: Collaborative programme for this Avion de Transport Regional (hence ATR) between Aérospatiale (France) and Aeritalia—now Alenia—(Italy) was launched in October 1981, with final assembly by former. The ATR 42–200 is the basic initial version. ATR 42–300 has same overall dimensions but operates at higher gross weight of 34,725 lb (15 750 kg) to carry bigger passenger payload in high-density layout. PW121 engines are optional in ATR 42-320. Freighter version is designated ATR 42-F. Stretched-fuselage ATR 72 is separately described.

11

AEROSPATIALE/ALENIA ATR 42

Dimensions: Span, 80 ft 7½ in (24,57 m); length, 74 ft 4½ in (22,67 m); height, 24 ft 10¾ in (7,59 m); wing area, 586.6 sq ft (54,5 m²).
Weights: Operating weight empty, 21,986 lb (9 973 kg); max payload, 9,980 lb (4 527 kg); max fuel, 9,920 lb (4 500 kg); max take-off, 34,725 lb (15 750 kg); max landing, 34,171 lb (15 500 kg).

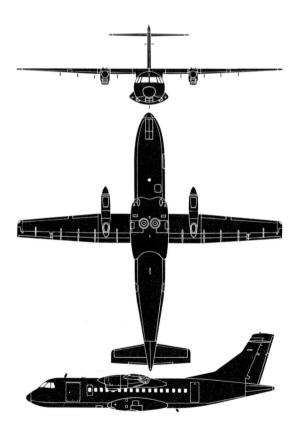

AEROSPATIALE/ALENIA ATR 72

Dimensions: Span, 88 ft 9 in (27,05 m); overall length 89 ft 1½ in (27,17 m); overall height, 25 ft 1 in (7,65 m); wing area, 657 sq ft (61,0 m²).

Weights: Operating weight empty, 26,895 lb (12 200 kg); max payload, 15,765 lb (7 150 kg); max fuel, 11,025 lb (5 000 kg); max take-off, 44,070 lb (19 990 kg); max landing, 43,870 lb (19 900 kg); max zero fuel, 42,660 lb (19 350 kg).

AEROSPATIALE/ALENIA ATR 72

Country of Origin: France and Italy.

Type: Short-range regional airliner.

Power Plant: Two Pratt & Whitney Canada PW124B turboprops, each flat rated at 2,400 shp (1 790 kW) for take-off.

Performance: Max cruising speed, 286 kts (530 km/h) at 25,000 ft (7 620 m); economical cruise, 248 kts (460 km/h) at 25,000 ft (7 620 m); range with max payload, 645 naut mls (1 195 km); range with max fuel, 2,370 naut mls (4 390 km).

Accommodation: Flight crew of two. Typical layout for 66 passengers, four-abreast. Max seating for 74, four-abreast at 30-in (76-cm) seat pitch.

Status: Two aircraft for development flown on 27 October and 20 December 1988. Third aircraft flown April 1989 and delivered to Kar Air in Finland as first customer aircraft following French certification September 1989.

Sales: 121 on firm order and 85 on option. 18 delivered by January 1991.

Notes: ATR 72 was developed as a stretched ATR 42 with lengthened fuselage and extended wing span. An optional version has higher gross weight of 47,400 lb (21 500 kg) and a range of 1,440 naut mls (2 666 km) with 66 passengers. The ATR 72-210, launched in 1990, is powered by uprated PW127 engines for 'hot and high' operations and is the version featured in the large order placed by AMR on behalf of American Eagle. Freight-carrying and military versions are available.

AEROSPATIALE/BAe CONCORDE

Country of Origin: United Kingdom and France.

Type: Medium-range supersonic transport.

Power Plant: Four 38,050 lb st (169,1 kN) Rolls-Royce (Bristol)/ SNECMA Olympus 593 Mk 610 reheated turbojets.

Performance: Max cruise, 1,176 kts (2 179 km/h) at 51,300 ft (15 635 m); range with max payload, 3,360 naut mls (6 230 km); range with max fuel, 3,550 naut mls (6 580 km).

Accommodation: Flight crew of three and 128 passengers four-abreast with central aisle at 34-in (86-cm) pitch; maximum, 144 passengers.

Status: Prototypes 001 and 002 first flown on 2 March 1969 (Toulouse) and 9 April 1969 (Filton); pre-production 01 and 02 first flown 17 December 1971 (Toulouse) and 10 January 1973 (Filton). First two production Concordes flown 6 December 1973 (Toulouse) and 13 February 1974 (Filton). Certification 13 October 1975 (France) and 5 December 1975 (UK); first revenue services 21 January 1976 (Air France and BOAC). Last production aircraft flown, 26 December 1978 (Toulouse) and 20 April 1979 (Filton).

Sales: Seven each to Air France and British Airways; first two production aircraft not brought up to full delivery standard.

Notes: Concorde is to date the only supersonic transport successfully put into airline service, although its operation has to be subsidized by British and French governments. Services have been flown on routes to the Middle and Far East and across the South Atlantic, but since 1983 the London and Paris routes to New York and Washington have been the only ones flown regularly by the two airlines, with the BA route extended from Washington to Miami in March 1984. Charter flights take Concorde to many other parts of the world.

AEROSPATIALE/BAe CONCORDE

Dimensions: Span, 83 ft 10 in (25,56 m); length, 203 ft 9 in (62,17 m); height, 37 ft 5 in (11,40 m); wing area, 3,856 sq ft (358,25 m²).
Weights: Operating empty, 189,400 lb (85 900 kg); max payload, 28,000 lb (12 700 kg); max take-off, 408,000 lb (185 070 kg); max landing, 245,000 lb (111 130 kg).

AIRBUS A300

Dimensions: Span, 147 ft 1 in (44,84 m); length, 177 ft 5 in (54,08 m); height, 54 ft 6½ in (16,62 m); gross wing area, 2,798.6 sq ft (260,0 m²).
Weights (-600): Operating weight empty, 190,100 lb (86 240 kg); max fuel, 129,200 lb (58 604 kg); max payload, 96,500 lb (43 770 kg); max take-off, 378,535 lb (171 700 kg); max landing, 308,640 lb (140 000 kg); max zero fuel, 271,160 lb (123 000 kg).

AIRBUS A300

Country of Origin: International.

Type: Medium-to-long-range large-capacity transport.

Power Plant (-600): Two Pratt & Whitney PW4000 or General Electric CF6-80C2 turbofans, thrust class 56,000–61,500 lb st (249–273,6 kN) according to variant.

Performance (-600R): Max cruise, 484 kts (897 km/h) at 30,000 ft (7 620 m); economical cruise, 472 kts (875 km/h) at 31,000 ft (9 450 m); max operating altitude, 40,000 ft (12 200 m); range with max passenger payload (267 pax), 4,340 naut mls (8 043 km); range with max fuel (payload 65,500 lb/29 710 kg), 5,100 naut mls (9 450 km).

Accommodation: Two pilots. Typical two-class layout for 28F + 239E. Max passengers, 375, nine-abreast at 28/30-in (71/76-cm) pitch.

Status: A300B1 prototypes flown on 28 October 1972 and 5 February 1973. First B2 flown 28 June 1973, certificated 15 March 1974, entered service (Air France) 23 May 1974. First B4 flown 26 December 1974; first with P & W engines flown 28 April 1979; first with FFCC flown 6 October 1981. First -600 flown 8 July 1983, certificated 9 March 1984, entered service (Saudia) April 1984; first with GE engines flown 20 March 1985. First -600R flown 9 December 1987, certificated 10 March 1988, entered service April 1988 (American Airlines).

Sales: Total of 417 (all A300 variants) sold to 48 customers. 340 delivered by February 1991.

Notes: The A300 is manufactured by a consortium of Aérospatiale (France), Deutsche Aerospace (Germany) and British Aerospace (UK), with small shares held by Fokker (Netherlands) and CASA (Spain). The A300B4-100 was heavier longer-range version of original A300B2-100. B4-200 had further weight increase and A300-600, which, with the -600R, was the only variant remaining in production in 1990, had redesigned rear fuselage, wing modifications and other improvements for better economy. A300-600R was similar with a tailplane fuel tank, PW4000 engine option, winglets and higher gross weight options. The A300C4 has a side-loading cargo door. *Photo:* A300-600R.

AIRBUS A310

Country of Origin: International.
Type: Short-to-medium-range large-capacity transport.
Power Plant: Two Pratt & Whitney PW4000 or General Electric CF6-80C2 turbofans, thrust class 52,000–53,500 lb st (231,3–238 kN) according to variant.
Performance (-300): Max cruise, 484 kts (897 km/h) at 35,000 ft (10 670 m); economical cruise, 459 kts (850 km/h) at 37,000 ft (11 300 m); max operating altitude, 41,000 ft (12 500 m); range with 218 passengers, 4,950 naut mls (9 175 km); range with max fuel (payload 53,850 lb/24 400 kg), 5,100 naut mls (9 500 km).
Accommodation: Two pilots. Typical two-class layout for 20F + 198E. Max passengers 280, nine-abreast at 30-in (76-cm).
Status: First two -200 aircraft (P & W engines) flown 3 April and 13 May 1982; first with GE engines 5 August 1982; certificated 11 March 1983, entered service (Lufthansa) 12 April 1983. First -200 with wing fences delivered (Thai Airways) 7 May 1986. First -200C convertible delivered (Martinair) 29 November 1984. First -300 flown (P & W engines) 8 July 1985, certificated 5 December 1985, entered service (Swissair) December 1985. First flight with GE engines 6 September 1985, certification and delivery (Air India) April 1986. First flight with PW4000s 8 November 1986, certification June 1987.
Sales: Total of 252 (all A310 variants) sold to 44 customers.
Notes: A310 is a reduced-capacity derivative of the A300, featuring a shortened fuselage, brand-new wing, updated systems and application of new materials where suitable. Basic aircraft is the A310-200 (CF6 engines) or -220 (JT9D engines); higher weight options of these are also on offer. The A310-300 carries an extra 15,430 lb (7 000 kg) of fuel in the tailplane to increase the range, and has higher maximum take-off weight as shown here. A310C convertible and A310F all-freight versions are available. *Photo:* A310-300.

AIRBUS A310-300

Dimensions: Span, 144 ft 0 in (43,89 m); length, 153 ft 1 in (46,66 m); height, 51 ft 10 in (15,80 m); gross wing area, 2,357.3 sq ft (219,0 m²). **Weights** (-300): Operating weight empty, 175,800 lb (79 700 kg); max fuel, 108,090 lb (42 029 kg); max payload, 75,500 lb (34 300 kg); max take-off, 346,100 lb (157 000 kg); max landing, 273,375 lb (124 000 kg); max zero fuel, 251,330 lb (114 000 kg).

AIRBUS A320

Dimensions: Span, 111 ft 9½ in (34,09 m); overall length, 123 ft 3 in (37,57 m); overall height, 38 ft 8½ in (11,80 m); gross wing area, 1,320 sq ft (123 m²).
Weights: Operating weight empty, 91,050 lb (41,300 kg); max fuel, 42,238 lb (19 159 kg); max payload, 105,600 lb (47 900 kg); max take-off, 162,040 lb (73 500 kg); max landing, 142,195 lb (64 500 kg); max zero fuel, 133,380 lb (60 500 kg).

AIRBUS A320

Country of Origin: International.

Type: Short-to-medium-range jetliner.

Power Plant: Two 25,000 lb st (111.2 kN) CFM56-5-A1 or IAE V2500-A1 turbofans.

Performance (A320-200): Max cruise, 487 kts (903 km/h) at 28,000 ft (8 530 m); economical cruise, 454 kts (840 km/h) at 37,000 ft (11 280 m); range with max payload (150 passengers), 2,930 naut mls (5 430 km).

Accommodation: Flight crew of two. Typical two-class layout for 12 + 138. One-class layout for 164 at 32-in (81-cm) pitch. Maximum seating 179.

Status: Four flight test and development aircraft (with CFM56 engines) flown 22 February, 27 April, 18 June and 8 July 1987 respectively. Certification (-100 standard) 26 February 1988. First -100 delivery (Air France) 28 March 1988. Certification (-200 standard) 8 November 1988. First flight with V2500 engines 28 July 1988, certification 20 April 1989, first delivery (Adria Airways) 18 May 1989. First flight A321 March 1993.

Sales: Orders for 658 A320s from 32 customers by February 1991.

Notes: A320 was launched into development and production in March 1984 when British and German financial participation was agreed by respective governments, to add to French government support already authorized. Major work shares are: Aérospatiale, 34 per cent, Deutsche Aerospace, 35 per cent, British Aerospace, 24 per cent, CASA, 5 per cent and Belairbus (Belgium), 2 per cent. The A320-200 described above is standard version, superseding the A320-100 (21 built) with less fuel, lower weights and without winglets. A321, launched in 1989, has lengthened fuselage (see following pages).

AIRBUS A321

Country of Origin: International.
Type: Short-to-medium-range jetliner.
Power Plant: Two 31,500 lb st (140 kN) CFM56-5B or 30,000 lb st (133,5 kN) IAE V2530-A5 turbofans.
Performance: Max cruising speed, 487 kts (902 km/h) at 28,000 ft (8 535 m); economical cruise, 447 kts (828 km/h) at 37,000 ft (11 278 m); range with full passenger payload, 2,350 naut mls (4 350 km); range with max fuel, 3,130 naut mls (5 800 km).
Accommodation: Flight crew of two. Typical two-class layout for 16 + 170 passengers. Max seating for 220, six-abreast at 29-in (73-cm) seat pitch.
Status: Launched November 1989. First flight scheduled March 1993 with four aircraft used for development/certification, covering both engine types by early 1994.
Sales: Total of 137 ordered by February 1991, for ten customers.
Notes: The A321 was launched as the first stretch of the A320 (see previous pages), with the full industrial launch in November 1989 following a marketing launch in May that had demonstrated a satisfactory market demand. Two fuselage 'plugs', ahead of and behind the wing, increase the fuselage length by 14 ft (4,27 m), allowing 36 more passengers to be carried, in six rows. Minimum changes for the extra length and higher weights include a strengthened undercarriage, uprated engines and modified wing trailing edge with double slotted flaps.

AIRBUS A321

Dimensions: Span, 111 ft 9½ in (34,09 m); overall length, 146 ft 0 in (44,5 m); overall height, 38 ft 8½ in (11,8 m); wing area, 1,320 sq ft (123 m²).

Weights: Operating weight empty, 103,500 lb (46 900 kg); max payload, 48,600 lb (22 000 kg); max fuel, 41,970 lb (19 040 kg); max take-off, 181,200 lb (82 200 kg); max landing, 160,900 lb (73 000 kg); max zero fuel, 152,100 lb (69 000 kg).

AIRBUS A330

Dimensions: Span, 197 ft 8 in (60,3 m); length, 208 ft 10 in (63,65 m); height, 55 ft 1 in (16,8 m); gross wing area, 3,910 sq ft (363 m²).
Weights: Operating weight empty, 261,300 lb (118 500 kg); max fuel, 165,300 lb (75 000 kg); max payload, 100,300 lb (45 500 kg); max take-off, 467,400 lb (212 000 kg); max landing, 383,600 lb (174 000 kg); max zero fuel, 360,450 lb (163 500 kg).

AIRBUS A330

Country of Origin: International.

Type: Medium-to-long-range large-capacity jetliner.

Power Plant: Two General Electric CF6-80E1 or Pratt & Whitney PW4000 or Rolls-Royce RB211 Trent turbofans, thrust class 64,000–72,000 lb st (284–320 kN).

Performance: Max cruise, 493 kts (914 km/h) at 37,000 ft (11 300 m); economical cruise, 470 kts (871 km/h) at 40,000 ft (12 200 m); max operating altitude, 41,000 ft (12 500 m); range with 335 pax, 4,750 naut mls (8 800 km); range with max fuel (payload 38,500 lb/17 500 kg), 6,300 naut mls (11 700 km).

Accommodation: Two pilots. Typical two-class layout for 30F + 305E. Max passengers 440, nine abreast at 30-in (76-cm) pitch.

Status: A330 launched June 1987 as large-capacity medium/long-range twin-engined variant of four-engined A340. First flight autumn 1992, certification autumn 1993, entry into service (Air Inter) September 1993.

Sales: Total commitments (firm orders), 138 for 13 customers by February 1991.

Notes: A330 uses same wing as A340, the two types having been launched coincidentally with the minimum structural changes for two or four engines. Fuselage is identical with that of the 'long' A340-300. Initial deliveries will be with CF6-80E1 engines; customers to date have also specified PW4000s and Rolls-Royce Trents, the latter being first application of R-R engines to an Airbus aircraft. First customer for the Trent-engined A330 is Cathay Pacific, which ordered 10 (with options on 10) announced in April 1989. Airbus has already planned to introduce an A330–300X version, allowing the range to grow to about 5,300 naut mls (9 800 km), with more powerful engines and gross weight of 491,600 lb (223 000 kg). The A330-400X is under study with a 21-ft (6,35-m) fuselage stretch, for 379 passengers in a two-class layout, at the same weight as the A330-300X and for 1997 delivery.

AIRBUS A340

Country of Origin: International.

Type: Very long-range large-capacity jetliner.

Power Plant: Four CFM International CFM56-5C-2 turbofans each rated at 31,200 lb st (140 kN) for take-off.

Performance (-200): Max cruise, 493 kts (914 km/h) at 37,000 ft (11 300 m); economical cruise, 470 kts (871 km/h) at 40,000 ft (12 200 m); max operating altitude, 41,000 ft (12 500 m); range with 262 pax, 7,550 naut mls (14 000 km); range with max fuel (payload 57,900 lb/26 250 kg), 8,000 naut mls (14 800 km).

Accommodation: Two pilots. Typical three-class layout for 18F + 74B + 170E. Max passengers 375, nine-abreast at 32-in (81-cm) pitch.

Status: A340 launched June 1987. First flight (-200) October 1991; first flight (-300) early 1992. First deliveries (Lufthansa and UTA) late 1992.

Sales: Total commitment (firm orders), 89 for 12 customers by February 1991.

Notes: A340/A330 duo, launched coincidentally, are largest aircraft to achieve production in Europe. A340-200 is very long-range version; A340-300 is lengthened by two fuselage frames, trading range for extra seats, and has projected maximum capacity of 440 passengers at 30-in (76-cm) pitch. Convertible versions will be available, with side door, and Airbus plans an A340-300X version, with 34,000 lb st (151 kN) CFM56-5C-4 engines and gross weight of 588,600 lb (267 000 kg), that will have a range of 7,150 naut mls (13 250 km). Production of first major A340 sections began in 1989, with first wing centre section completed at Nantes in November. Final assembly at Colomiers, near Toulouse, will take place in new facilities that are being provided by Aérospatiale.

AIRBUS A340

Dimensions: Span, 197 ft 8 in (60,3 m); length, (-200), 194 ft 10 in (59,39 m); height, 55 ft 1 in (16,8 m); gross wing area, 3,910 sq ft (363 m²).

Weights (-200): Operating weight empty, 269,200 lb (122 100 kg); max fuel, 238,500 lb (108 200 kg); max payload, 103,400 lb (46 900 kg); max take-off, 558,900 lb (253 500 kg); max landing, 399,000 lb (181 000 kg); max zero fuel, 372,600 lb (169 000 kg).

AIRTECH CN-235

Dimensions: Span, 84 ft 8 in (25,81 m); overall length, 70 ft 0¾ in (21,35 m); overall height, 26 ft 10 in (8,18 m); wing area, 636.1 sq ft (59,0 m²).

Weights (Srs 100): Operating weight empty, 20,725 lb (9 400 kg); max payload, 9,260 lb (4 200 kg); max fuel, 9,325 lb (4 320 kg); max take-off, 33,290 lb (15 100 kg); max landing, 33,180 lb (15 050 kg); max zero fuel, 29,980 lb (13 600 kg).

AIRTECH CN-235

Country of Origin: Spain and Indonesia.

Type: Twin turboprop regional airliner.

Power Plant: Two General Electric CT7-9C turboprops each flat rated at 1,750 shp (1 305 kW) for take-off and 1,870 shp (1 395 kW) with APR.

Performance (Srs 100): Max cruising speed, 244 kts (452 km/h) at 15,000 ft (4 575 m); range with max payload, 208 naut mls (385 km); range with max fuel, 2,110 naut mls (3 910 km).

Accommodation: Flight crew of two. Max seating for 45, four-abreast at 30-in (76-cm) seat pitch.

Status: First of two prototypes flown in Spain on 11 November 1983 and second in Indonesia on 31 December 1983. First flight of initial production aircraft on 19 August 1986, with Spanish and Indonesian certification on 20 June 1986 and full FAA certification on 3 December 1986. First production delivery (to Merpati Nusantara), 15 December 1986. First commercial operation (by Merpati), 1 March 1988.

Sales: Total orders for about 150 include some 60 for airline use, primarily in Spain and Indonesia.

Notes: Airtech (Aircraft Technology Industries) is jointly owned by CASA and IPTN to manage production and sales of CN-235, designed and built by those two companies with assembly lines in Spain and Indonesia. Early production aircraft were powered by CT7-5 engines and had lower operating weights. Srs 100 designation refers to CT7-9C engines and data as quoted here.

ANTONOV AN-24 and AN-30

Country of Origin: Soviet Union.

Type: Regional and special duty transport.

Power Plant: Two (An-24V) 2,530 ehp (1 887 kW) Ivchenko AI-24A or (An-26, An-30), 2,820 ehp (2 103 kW) AI-24VT turboprops.

Performance (An-24V): Max cruise, 269 kts (498 km/h); best-range cruise, 243 kts (450 km/h) at 19,700 ft (6 000 m); range with max payload, 296 naut mls (550 km); range with max fuel, 1,293 naut mls (2 400 km).

Accommodation: Flight crew of up to five (two pilots, flight engineer, navigator and radio operator), but normally three for passenger-carrying flights. Up to 50 passengers, four abreast.

Status: An-24 prototype first flown April 1960. Service use (by Aeroflot) began in September 1963. Production completed.

Sales: Production total about 1,100 An-24s in all versions, primarily for Aeroflot and export to airlines of all Eastern Bloc countries in Europe and to Air Guinee, Air Mali, Cubana, CAAC in China, Egyptair, Iraqi Airways, etc.

Notes: The An-24 was the first Soviet transport to apply turboprop power for short-haul operations and proved among the most successful, remaining in production for some 15 years. Original basic An-24 was followed by improved An-24V; An-24T was a specialized freighter, and An-24RT and improved An-24RV had an auxiliary turbojet in the starboard nacelle to boost take-off. An-24P was developed for fire fighting and the An-30, which appeared in 1973, had a new front fuselage and was equipped for air survey and map-making. The An-26, with a rear-loading ramp, was developed and produced primarily for military use, as was the An-32 with 5,180 ehp (3 862 kW) Ivchenko AI-20M engines. *Photo:* An-24RV.

ANTONOV AN-24

Dimensions: Span, 95 ft 9½ in (29,20 m); length, 77 ft 2½ in (23,53 m); height, 27 ft 3½ in (8,32 m); wing area, 807.1 sq ft (74,98 m²).
Weights: Empty equipped, 29,320 lb (13 300 kg); max payload, 12,125 lb (5 500 kg); max fuel, 10,494 lb (4 760 kg); max take-off and landing, 46,300 lb (21 000 kg).

ANTONOV AN-28

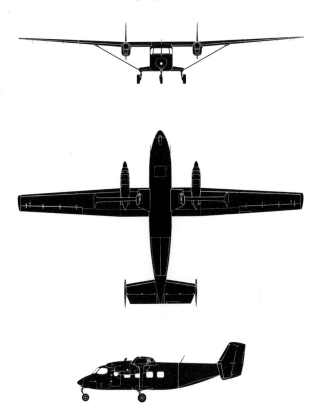

Dimensions: Span, 72 ft 4½ in (22,07 m); length, 42 ft 11¾ in (13,10 m); height, 16 ft 1 in (4,90 m); wing area, 427.5 sq ft (39,72 m²).
Weights: Empty equipped, 8,600 lb (3 900 kg); max payload, 4,410 lb (2 000 kg); max fuel, 3,371 lb (1 529 kg); max take-off and landing, 14,330 lb (6 500 kg); max zero fuel weight, 12,972 lb (5 884 kg).

ANTONOV AN-28

Country of Origin: Soviet Union/Poland.

Type: Light general purpose transport.

Power Plant: Two 960 shp (716 kW) Polish-built (PZL Rzeszow) Glushenkov TVD-10B (PZL-10S) turboprops.

Performance: Max cruising speed, 189 kts (350 km/h) at 9,850 ft (3 000 m); economical cruising speed, 181 kts (335 km/h); range with max payload (20 passengers), 275 naut mls (510 km); range with max fuel, 736 naut mls (1 365 km).

Accommodation: Flight crew of one or two; typical seating for 15 passengers three-abreast at 28-in (72-cm) pitch with offset aisle, or maximum high-density seating for 20.

Status: Prototype An-28 first flown in Soviet Union September 1969 (with TVD-850 engines). Pre-production An-28 first flown April 1975 after being re-engined with TVD-10Bs. First production aircraft flown in Poland, 22 July 1984. Soviet certification, 7 February 1986.

Sales: Soviet Union has stated a requirement for 1,200. More than 120 delivered by early 1991 (including some military).

Notes: The An-28 was selected in the late 'seventies after a 'fly-off' against the Beriev Be-30, to meet Soviet requirements for a light general utility aircraft that could supplement or replace the many hundreds of An-2s and An-14s operating as transports. The prototype was at first known as the An-14M and it shares with the An-14 a high-wing layout with twin fins and rudders, but differs in having a much-enlarged fuselage and turboprop engines. The latter were at first TVD-850s but the more powerful TVD-10Bs have been adopted for the production An-28. The PZL Mielec factory in Poland has sole responsibility for producing the An-28, initially to meet Soviet requirements reported to run into many hundreds of aircraft.

BEECHCRAFT 1900C AIRLINER

Country of Origin: USA.

Type: Twin turboprop regional airliner.

Power Plant: Two Pratt & Whitney Canada PT6A-65B turboprops, each flat-rated at 1,100 shp (820 kW) for take-off.

Performance: Max cruising speed, 267 kts (495 km/h) at 8,000 ft (2 440 m); and 254 kts (471 km/h) at 25,000 ft (7 620 m); range with 10-passenger payload, 1,570 naut mls (2 907 km).

Accommodation: Flight crew of one or two. Typical layout for 19 passengers, two-abreast.

Status: Prototypes first flown on 3 September and 30 November 1982, for performance and systems testing respectively. FAA certification on 22 November 1983. First delivery, February 1984. First flight of Model 1900D on 1 March 1990, for certification mid-1991.

Sales: Approximately 200 sold for airline use, principally in the US.

Notes: Beech Aircraft developed the 1900 Airliner as part of its commitment to re-enter this part of the market, after stopping production of the smaller Beech 99 in 1975. Two versions of the Super King Air 200 were studied—the Model 1300 with the standard fuselage and the 1900 with lengthened fuselage and uprated engines; the latter entered production as the Model 1900C airliner and, for business use, as the King Air Exec-Liner. A 'wet' wing containing an additional 204 Imp gal (927 l) of fuel became available for the 1900C in 1986. The Model 1900D, for introduction in 1991, features a new deepened fuselage with 'stand-up' headroom in the cabin, and winglets in addition to the 'tail-ets' on the tailplane tips and 'stabilons' on the lower rear fuselage that were adopted after initial wind-tunnel testing of the 1900 configuration. The engines of the 1900D are 1,280 shp (955 kW) PT6A-67Ds and gross weight is 16,950 lb (7 668 kg).

BEECHCRAFT 1900C AIRLINER

Dimensions: Span, 54 ft 5¾ in (16,60 m); overall length, 57 ft 10 in (17,63 m); overall height, 14 ft 10¾ in (4,54 m); wing area, 303 sq ft (28,15 m²).
Weights: Empty, 9,540 lb (4 327 kg); max fuel, 4,460 lb (2 027 kg); max take-off, 16,600 lb (7 530 kg); max landing, 16,100 lb (7 302 kg); max zero fuel, 14,000 lb (6 350 kg).

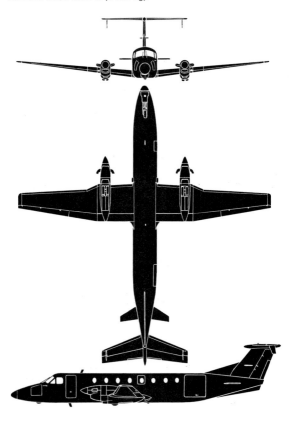

BOEING 707-320

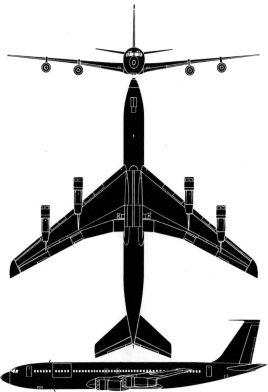

Dimensions: Span, 145 ft 8½ in (44,42 m); length, 152 ft 11 in (45,60 m); height, 42 ft 5½ in (12,94 m); wing area, 3,050 sq ft (283,4 m²).

Weights (707-320B): Operating weight empty, 146,400 lb (66 406 kg); max payload, 53,900 lb (24 450 kg); max fuel, 159,560 lb (72 375 kg); max zero fuel, 230,000 lb (104 330 kg); max take-off, 333,600 lb (151 315 kg); max landing, 247,000 lb (112 037 km).

BOEING 707-320

Country of Origin: USA.

Type: Long-range jet transport.

Power Plant: Four 18,000 lb st (80 kN) Pratt & Whitney JT3D-3 or 19,000 lb st (84,4 kN) JT3D-7 turbofans.

Performance (-320C): Max cruising speed, 525 kts (973 km/h) at 25,000 ft (7 620 m); long-range cruise, 464 kts (860 km/h) at 35,000 ft (10 670 m); range with max passenger payload, 3,735 naut mls (6 920 km); range with max fuel and 147 passengers, 5,000 naut mls (9 265 km).

Accommodation: Flight crew of three or four and up to 189 passengers six-abreast with central aisle at a pitch of 32-in (81-cm).

Status: First 707-320 flown 11 January 1959, certificated 15 July 1959, entered service (Pan American) 26 August 1959. First 707-420 flown 20 May 1959, certificated (USA) 12 February and (UK) 27 April 1960; entered service (BOAC) May 1960. First 707-320B flown 31 January 1962, certificated 31 May 1962, entered service (Pan American) June 1962. First 707-320C flown 19 February 1963, certificated 30 April 1963, entered service (Pan American) June 1963. Production complete (except military variants).

Sales: Overall 707-320/720 sales total by end 1990, 1,010, of which 132 military or non-commercial. Commercial 707-320 sales totalled 69 and 707-420, 37; 707-320B/-320C sales for commercial use totalled 482.

Notes: The Intercontinental 707-320 emerged as a longer version of the 707-120 with extra wing area, at first with turbojets but in its ·320B and (with cargo door) -320C versions, with turbofans. Some 215 Boeing 707s were in airline service in 1990, mostly -320Bs and -320Cs. *Photo:* Boeing 707-3J6C.

BOEING 727

Country of Origin: USA.

Type: Short-medium-range jet transport.

Power Plant: Three 14,500 lb st (64,4 kN) Pratt & Whitney JT8D-9A or 15,500 lb st (68,9 kN) JT8D-15 or 16,000 lb st (71,1 kN) JT8D-17 or 17,400 lb st (77,3 kN) JT8D-17R (with automatic thrust reserve) turbofans.

Performance: Max cruise, 530 kts (982 km/h) at 25,000 ft (7 620 m); economical cruise, 467 kts (865 km/h); range with max payload, 2,140 naut mls (3 966 km); range with max fuel, 2,400 naut mls (9 447 km).

Accommodation: Flight crew of three and up to 189 passengers six-abreast with central aisle, at 30-in (76-cm) seat pitch.

Status: First 727-100 flown on 9 February 1963, certificated on 24 December 1963 and entered service (Eastern Airlines) on 1 February and (United) 6 February 1964. First 727C (with cargo door and handling system) flown 30 December 1964, certificated 13 January 1966, entered service (Northwest Orient) 23 April 1966. First 727-200 flown 27 July 1967, certificated 29 November 1967, entered service (Northeast Airlines) 14 December 1967. First Advanced 727 flown 3 March 1972, certificated 14 June 1972, entered service (All Nippon Airways) July 1972. First flight with automatic thrust reserve (ATR), 27 May 1976. First -200F flown 28 April 1983. First Valsan -200A conversion flown 12 July 1988. Last aircraft delivered 18 September 1984.

Sales: Grand total of 1,831 Boeing 727s sold includes 1,249 727-200 and Advanced 727-200s.

Notes: To allow early 727 variants to meet 1990 noise limits, Valsan Partners offers a retrofit package that puts JT8D-217C turbofans in outboard nacelles. United Parcel Service has ordered a Rolls-Royce Tay retrofit by Dee Howard for its fleet of 727-100s. *Photo: 727-2B7.*

BOEING 727

Dimensions: Span, 108 ft 0 in (32,92 m); length, 153 ft 2 in (46,69 m); height, 34 ft 0 in (10,36 m); wing area, 1,700 sq ft (157,9 m²).

Weights (-200): Operating weight empty (typical), 101,773 lb (46 164 kg); max payload, 41,000 lb (18 594 kg); standard fuel, 54,010 lb (24 498 kg); max fuel, 59,750 lb (27 102 kg); max take-off, 184,800–209,500 lb (83 820–95 027 kg); max landing, 154,500–161,000 lb (70 080–73 028 kg).

BOEING 737-200

Dimensions: Span, 93 ft 0 in (28,35 m); length, 100 ft 2 in (30,53 m); height, 37 ft 0 in (11,28 m); wing area, 980 sq ft (91,04 m²).
Weights: Operating weight empty (typical), 61,050 lb (27 691 kg); max fuel, 39,855 lb (18,078 kg); max take-off, 115,500–128,100 lb (52 390–58 105 kg); max zero fuel, 95,000–99,000 lb (43 091–44 906 kg); max landing, 103,000–107,000 lb (46 720–48 534 kg).

BOEING 737-200

Country of Origin: USA.

Type: Short-to-medium-range jetliner.

Power Plant: Two 14,500 lb st (64,5 kN) Pratt & Whitney JT8D-9A or 15,500 lb st (68,95 kN) JT8D-15 or 16,000 lb st (71,17 kN) JT8D-17 or 17,400 lb st (77,40 kN) JT8D-17R (with automatic thrust reserve) turbofans.

Performance: Max cruise at mid-cruise weight, 500 kts (927 km/h) at 22,600 ft (6 890 m); economical cruise, 430 kts (796 km/h) at 30,000 ft (9 145 m); range (according to weight) with 115 passengers, 1,900–2,300 naut mls (3 521–4 262 km).

Accommodation: Flight crew of two or three, typical layout for 115 passengers, or up to 130 six-abreast at 29-in (74-cm) pitch.

Status: First 737-100 flown 9 April 1967; first 737-200 flown on 8 August 1967. Certification (-100) on 15 December 1967 and (-200) on 21 December 1967. Entered service (-100, Lufthansa) on 10 February 1968 and (-200, United) 28 April 1968. First advanced 737-200 flown on 15 April 1971, certificated 3 May and entered service (All Nippon Airways) June 1971.

Sales: Total of 29 -100s (plus 20 non-commercial), and 1,081 -200/ -200C (plus 14 non-commercial), making 1,144 'pre-300' Boeing 737s built. Production of -100/-200 completed mid-1988.

Notes: Original 737-100, launched in February 1965, was quickly superseded by the -200 with 6 ft (1,82 m) longer fuselage and many progressively-introduced improvements. Now succeeded by the re-engined -300/-400/-500 family (refer to next entries). *Photo:* 737-260.

BOEING 737-300 and -500

Country of Origin: USA.

Type: Short-to-medium-range jet transport.

Power Plant: Two (-500) 18,500 lb st (82,3 kN) CFM International CFM56-3B4 or (-300, -500) 20,000 lb st (89 kN) CFM56-3B1 or (-300) 22,000 lb st (97,9 kN) CFM56-3B2 turbofans.

Performance (-300): Max cruising speed, 491 kts (908 km/h) at 26,000 ft (7 925 m); long-range cruising speed, 429 kts (794 km/h) at 35,000 ft (10 670 m); range with 128 passengers and standard fuel, 1,815 naut mls (3 362 km); range with 128 passengers and max fuel, 2,685 naut mls (4 973 km).

Accommodation: Flight crew of two and up to 149 (-300) or 132 (-500) passengers six abreast with single aisle at 30-in (76-cm) pitch; typical mixed-class layout (-300) for eight first class and 120 tourist.

Status: Development and production go-ahead for -300 on 26 March 1981. Flight test aircraft first flown on 24 February, 2 March and 2 May 1984. FAA certification 14 November 1984, first deliveries 28 November (US Air) and 30 November (Southwest), first revenue service (Southwest), 7 December 1984. Srs 500 development aircraft flown 30 June 1989, certificated 12 February, first delivery (Southwest Airlines) 28 February 1990 and (Braathens SAFE) March 1990.

Sales: Total sales, Srs 300, 918; Srs 500, 229. Overall total of 1,741 sales of -300/-400/-500 includes 296 unspecified by variant.

Notes: The 300/400/500 family feature CFM56 engines and different fuselage lengths, with the -500 approximately equivalent to the -200 (previous entry) and -300 and -400 having greater seating capacities. See next entry for details of -400. *Photo:* Boeing 737-3H9.

BOEING 737-300 and -500

Dimensions: Span, 94 ft 9 in (28,88 m); length (-300), 109 ft 7 in (33,40 m); length (-500) 101 ft 9 in (31,0 m); height, 36 ft 6 in (11,13 m); wing area, 1,135 sq ft (105,4 m²).
Weights (-300): Operating weight empty, 69,580 lb (31 561 kg); max payload, 35,420 lb (16 067 kg); max take-off, 124,500–138,500 lb (56 473–62 882 kg); max landing, 114,000 lb (51 710 kg); max zero fuel weight, 105,000–106,500 lb (47 628–48 308 kg).

BOEING 737-400

Dimensions: Span, 94 ft 9 in (28,88 m); overall length, 119 ft 7 in (36,45 m); overall height, 36 ft 6 in (11,13 m); gross wing area, 1,135 sq ft (105,4 m²).
Weights: Operating weight empty, 73,790 lb (33 470 kg); max payload, 40,300 lb (18 280 kg); max take-off, 138,500–150,000 lb (62 822–68 039 kg); max landing, 121,000–124,000 lb (54 880–56 245 kg); max zero fuel, 113,000–117,000 lb (51 250–53 070 kg).

BOEING 737-400

Country of Origin: USA.

Type: Short-to-medium-range jetliner.

Power Plant: Two 22,000 lb st (97,86 kN) CFM International CFM56-3B-2 or 23,500 lb st (104,5 kN) CFM56-3C-1 turbofans.

Performance: Max cruise, 492 kts (912 km/h) at mid-cruise weight at 26,000 ft (10 670 m); economical cruise, 439 kts (813 km/h) at 30,000 ft (9 150 m); max operating altitude, 37,000 ft (11 278 m); range with max payload (146 passengers), 2,160 naut mls (4 003 km); range with max payload (high gross weight option), 2,550 naut mls (4 723 km).

Accommodation: Flight crew of two. Typical two-class seating for 8 + 138 and one-class for 159, six-abreast at 32-in (81-cm) pitch. Max seating 188.

Status: Srs 400 development aircraft flown 19 February and 25 March 1988, certificated 2 September, first delivery (Piedmont) 15 September 1988. First high-gross weight model rolled out 23 December 1988.

Sales: Total orders for 298 by early 1991, for 26 customers. Overall total of 1,741 sales of -300/-400/-500 includes 296 unspecified by variant.

Notes: The 737-400 was announced by Boeing in June 1986 as a stretched variant of the 737-300 (see previous entry), with which it shared the new CFM56 power plant installation. It is the longest of the trio of 737 variants in production in 1991, a fact reflected in the fitting, as standard, of a tail bumper as protection in the event of over-rotation during take-off. The high gross weight option requires strengthened wing and landing gear. *Photo:* Boeing 737-4Y0.

BOEING 747-200

Country of Origin: USA.

Type: Long-range large-capacity jet transport.

Power Plant: Four Pratt & Whitney JT9D, General Electric CF6-50E2 or CF6-80C2 or Rolls-Royce RB211–524D turbofans, thrust class 52,500–56,700 lb st (233,5–252,2 kN) according to variant.

Performance (-200B): Max cruise, 507 kts (981 km/h) at 35,000 ft (10 670 m); economical cruise, 490 kts (907 km/h) at 35,000 ft (10 670 m); range with 366 pax, 6,900 naut mls (12 778 km).

Accommodation: Flight crew of three. Typical two-class layout for 32F and 420E. Max passengers 550, eleven-abreast.

Status: First 747 flown 9 February 1969, certificated 30 December 1969, entered service (Pan Am), 22 January 1970. First -200 flown 11 October 1970, certificated 23 December 1970. First 747F flown 30 November 1971, certificated 7 March 1972. First 747C flown 23 March 1973, certificated 24 April 1973. First 747SR flown 4 September, delivered 26 September 1973. First 747SP flown 4 July 1975, certificated 4 February 1976.

Sales: Total of 643 Srs 100 and Srs 200, comprising 43SP; 167 -100; nine -100B; 29 -100SR; 224 -200B; 13 -200C; 69 -200F; 77 -200M and 12 non-commercial aircraft.

Notes: Srs 100 and Srs 200 have same dimensions, different weight and engine options, different equipment standards. SP = Special Performance, with shorter fuselage. SR = Short Range. B = improvements for higher weights. C = Convertible. F = Freighter. C = Combi with side door. *Photo:* Boeing 747-238B.

BOEING 747-200

Dimensions: Span, 195 ft 8 in (59,64 m); length, 231 ft 10 in (70,66 m); height, 63 ft 5 in (19,33 m); gross wing area, 5,500 sq ft (511 m²).

Weights (-200): Operating weight empty, 380,800 lb (172 728 kg); max fuel, 361,870 lb (164 141 kg); max payload, 145,700 lb (66 088 kg); max take-off, 833,000 lb (377 840 kg); max landing, 630,000 lb (285 765 kg); max zero fuel, 526,500 lb (238 815 kg).

BOEING 747-300 and -400

Dimensions: Span, 211 ft 0 in (64,31 m); length, 231 ft 10 in (70,66 m); height, 63 ft 5 in (19,33 m); gross wing area 5,650 sq ft (525,0 m²).

Weights (-400): Operating weight empty, 390,700 lb (177 218 kg); max fuel, 384,824 lb (174 533 kg); max payload, 143,800 lb (65 230 kg); max take-off, 870,000 lb (394 625 kg); max landing, 630,000 lb (285 765 kg); max zero fuel, 535,000 lb (242 670 kg).

BOEING 747-300 and -400

Country of Origin: USA.

Type: Very long-range, large-capacity jet transport.

Power Plant: Four General Electric CF6-50E2 or CF6-80C2, or Pratt & Whitney JT9D or PW4000, or Rolls-Royce RB211-524D4 or -524G turbofans, thrust class 52,500–58,000 lb st (233,5–258 kN).

Performance (-400): Max speed, 532 kts (985 km/h) at 30,000 ft (9 150 m); max operating altitude, 45,000 ft (13 716 m); range with 412 pax, 7,300 naut mls (13 528 km); range with max fuel (payload 94,800 lb/43 040 kg), 7,600 naut mls (14 100 km).

Accommodation: Two pilots. Typical three-class layout for 34F + 76B + 302E passengers. Max passengers 660, eleven abreast at 34-in (86-cm) pitch.

Status: First Srs 300 (JT9D engines) flew 5 October 1982, first with GE engines 10 December 1982, certification 7 March 1983, entry into service (Swissair) 28 March 1983. First Srs 400 (PW4000 engines) flown on 29 April 1988, first with CF6-80C2s on 27 June 1988, first with RB211s on 28 August 1988; certification 9 January 1989 and entry into service (Northwest Airlines).

Sales: Total of 81 Srs 300 and 399 Srs 400, comprising 55 -300; 21 -300M; four -300SR; 348 -400; 16 -400F; 33 -400M and three non-commercial.

Notes: Srs 300 introduced stretched upper deck on Srs 200B airframe. Srs 400 has extended wing tips with winglets (optional—as is extended upper deck—on -400F freighter), new range of engine options, modernised two-man cockpit and updated avionics and interior. Combi, freighter and SR versions available. *Photo:* Boeing 747-419.

BOEING 757

Country of Origin: USA.

Type: Short-medium-range jet transport.

Power Plant: Two 40,100 lb st (178,4 kN) Rolls-Royce RB211-535C or 40,100 lb st (178,4 kN) RB211-535E4 or 38,200 lb st (169,9 kN) Pratt & Whitney PW2037 or 41,700 lb st (185,7 kN) PW2040 turbofans.

Performance (Typical): Max cruise, 493 kts (914 km/h) at 37,000 ft (11 300 m); economical cruise, 459 kts (850 km/h) at 40,000 ft (12 200 m); range with 186 passengers and standard fuel, 2,780 naut mls (5 150 km); range with 186 passengers, high gross weight option, 3,910 naut mls (7 240 km).

Accommodation: Flight crew of two and up to 239 passengers six-abreast with central aisle at 32-in (81-cm) seat pitch; typical mixed class layout for 178 with four-abreast at 38-in (97-cm) pitch and six-abreast at 34-in (86-cm) pitch.

Status: First of five flight test and development aircraft flown on 19 February 1982 and second on 28 March 1982. Certification (FAA) 21 December 1982. First delivery 22 December 1982 and first service (Eastern) 1 January 1983. UK certification 14 January 1983 and first service (British Airways) 9 February 1983. First flight with PW2037 engines 14 March 1984, certificated October 1984, entry into service (Delta) November 1984. First 757PF flown mid-1987, certificated 3 September and entered service with UPS. First 757M Combi (Royal Nepal Airlines) flown 15 July 1988.

Sales: Total orders for 724, for 34 customers, comprising 664 -200 (one non-commercial), one -200M and 59 -200PF.

Notes: Boeing launched the 757 into full development and production on 23 March 1979. Earlier project activity had proceeded under the 7-N-7 generic title as Boeing searched for the correct formula for an aircraft designed to succeed the 727. The 757PF is a package freighter, with no cabin windows, designed for the small package carriers, and the 757M Combi has the same forward port side cargo door. The designation 77-52 applies to the Corporate version. *Photo:* Boeing 757-236.

BOEING 757

Dimensions: Span, 124 ft 10 in (38,05 m); length, 155 ft 3 in (47,32 m); height, 44 ft 6 in (13,56 m); wing area, 1,994 sq ft (185,25 m²).

Weights: Operating weight empty, 126,060 lb (57 180 kg); max fuel, 75,300 lb (34 150 kg); max payload, 57,530 lb (26 090 kg); max take-off, 220,000–255,000 lb (99 800–115 670 kg); max landing, 198,000 lb (89 810 kg); max zero fuel, 184,000 lb (83 460 kg).

BOEING 767-200

Dimensions: Span, 156 ft 1 in (47,57 m); length, 159 ft 2 in (48,51 m); height, 52 ft 0 in (15,85 m); gross wing area, 3,050 sq ft (283,3 m²).
Weights (-200): Operating weight empty, 177,500 lb (80 512 kg); max payload, 70,800 lb (32 115 kg); max fuel, 112,725 lb (51 131 kg); max take-off, 300,000–315,000 lb (136 078–142 900 kg); max landing, 272,000 lb (123 400 kg); max zero fuel, 250,000 lb (113 400 kg).

BOEING 767-200

Country of Origin: USA.

Type: Medium-to-long-range jet transport.

Power Plant: Two 48,000 lb st (213,5 kN) Pratt & Whitney JT9D-7R4D or 50,200 lb st (223,3 kN) PW4050 or (-200ER) 56,750 lb st (252,4 kN) PW4056 or 52,500 lb st (233,5 kN) General Electric CF6-80C2B2 or (-200ER) 57,900 lb st (257,7 kN) CF6-80C24B turbofans.

Performance: Max cruise, 493 kts (914 km/h) at 40,000 ft (12 200 m); economical cruise, 461 kts (854 km/h) at 35,000 ft (10 670 m); range with design payload (-200), 3,800 naut mls (7 040 km); (-200ER), 6,800 naut mls (12 600 km).

Accommodation: Two pilots. Typical two-class layout for 18F + 198E. Max passengers 290, eight abreast at 30-in (76-cm) pitch.

Status: First four -200s (JT9D engines) flown 26 September, 4 November, 28 and 30 December 1981; certification 30 July 1982, entered service (United) 8 September 1982. First with CF6 engines flown 19 February 1982, certificated 4 October, entered service (Delta) 15 December 1982. First -200ER (JT9Ds) flown 6 March 1984, delivered (Ethiopian Airlines) 23 May 1984.

Sales: Total of 222, comprising 128 -200s and 94 -200ERs (but see 767-300 next entry also). Total customers, all variants, 44.

Notes: Launched on 14 July 1978 after development as '7X7', Srs 200 is basic version; -200ER (extended range) has extra centre section tankage and take-off weights up to 387,000 lb (175 500 kg). *Photo:* Boeing 767-241ER.

BOEING 767-300

Country of Origin: USA.

Type: Medium-to-long-range jet transport.

Power Plant: Two 52,500–61,500 lb st (233,5–273,6 kN) General Electric CF6-80C2B or 50,200–60,000 lb st (223,3–266,9 kN) Pratt & Whitney PW4000 or 58,000–60,600 lb st (258,0–269,6 kN) Rolls-Royce RB211-524H turbofans.

Performance: Max cruise, 486 kts (900 km/h) at 39,000 ft (11 900 m); economical cruise, 459 kts (850 km/h) at 39,000 ft (11 900 m); range with design payload 4,000 naut mls (7 415 km); range with design payload, high gross weight option, 4,260 naut mls (7 895 km).

Accommodation: Two pilots. Typical three-class layout for 210. Max passengers 290, seven-abreast at 32-in (81-cm) pitch.

Status: First -300 (JT9D engines) flown 30 January 1986; certificated (JT9D and CF6-80A engines) 22 September 1986; first deliveries (JAL) September 1986. First -300ER (CF6-80C engines) flown 19 December 1986, certification and first deliveries (American Airlines) late 1987. First -300ER with RB211s flown May 1989, first deliveries (British Airways) 8 February 1990.

Sales: Total of 277, comprising 103 -300s, 174 -300ERs and 32 'to be decided' (could be -200 or -300).

Notes: Launched February 1983, the 767-300 has 21 ft 1 in (6,42 m) increase in fuselage length, higher weights and more powerful engine options than original -200 (previous entry). Extended range -300ER has more fuel and take-off weights up to 407,000 lb (184 600 kg), for ranges up to 6,000 naut mls (11 120 km). Projected 767-400 with further fuselage stretch did not proceed and was replaced by 767-X proposal, which was launched as the Boeing 777 in October 1990. *Photo:* Boeing 767-346.

BOEING 767-300

Dimensions: Span, 156 ft 1 in (47,57 m); length, 180 ft 3 in (54,94 m); height, 52 ft 0 in (15,85 m); gross wing area 3,050 sq ft (283,3 m²).
Weights: Operating weight empty, 179,400 lb (81 374 kg); max fuel, 112,725 lb (51 131 kg); max payload, 90,200 lb (40 915 kg); max take-off, 345,000–351,000 lb (156 490–159 210 kg); max landing, 300,000 lb (136 078 kg); max zero fuel, 288,000 lb (130 634 kg).

BOEING 777

Dimensions: Span, 196 ft 11 in (60,02 m); span (tips folded), 155 ft 9 in (47,47 m); overall length, 209 ft 1 in (63,73 m); overall height, 60 ft 2 in (18,33 m).

Weights: Max take-off (initial version), 506,000–515,000 lb (229 520–233 600 kg); max take-off (planned longer-range version), 580,000–590,000 lb (263 100–267 625 kg).

BOEING 777

Country of Origin: USA.

Type: Medium-to-long-range wide-body transport.

Power Plant: Two 73,100–84,500 lb st (325,2–375,9 kN) Pratt & Whitney PW4073/PW4082 or 72,000–85,000 lb st (320,3–378,1 kN) General Electric GE90 or 75,000–85,000 lb st (333,6–378,1 kN) Rolls-Royce Trent 871/872 turbofans.

Performance: Typical cruise, Mach = 0.83, 489 kts (905 km/h) at 30,000 ft (9 150 m); range with typical two-class (363-seat) payload, (initial version), 4,170–4,430 naut mls (7 700–8 200 km); (planned long-range version), 6,430–6,700 naut mls (11 900–12 400 km).

Accommodation: Flight crew of two. Typical two-class layout for 38F six-abreast and 325E 10-abreast with two aisles. Typical three class layout, 24F at 60-in (152-cm) pitch, 56B at 38-in (96,5-cm) pitch and 218E nine-abreast or 234E ten-abreast at 34-in (86,5-cm) pitch. Maximum accommodation, 440.

Status: First order placed 15 October 1990. Programme launch confirmed 29 October 1990. First flight June 1994. Deliveries begin in May 1995.

Sales: Launch order for 34, with 34 on option, by United Airlines (with PW4073 engines). Second order announced 19 December 1990, from All Nippon Airways for 15 (plus 10 on option).

Notes: Developed over a period of several years up to 1990 as the Model 767-X, the Boeing 777 as finally launched has little in common with the earlier type other than the overall configuration. Intended to fill the gap between the 767-300 and the 747-400, the Boeing 777 is conceived as a family of variants to cover medium-to-long ranges and featuring different fuselage lengths. The launch version (data above) is expected to be followed by a longer-range model some 18 months later, with weights of 580,000–590,000 lb (263 100–267 625 kg) and the ability to carry 300–320 passengers over 6,400 naut mls (11 850 km). Greater passenger capacity and more range will be offered in later versions. A unique feature, offered as an option, is the ability to fold the outer wing panels upwards, reducing the span by some 41 ft (12,5 m) in order to give the aircraft compatibility with existing gate and taxiway space at crowded airports.

BRITISH AEROSPACE 146-100 and -200

Country of Origin: United Kingdom.

Type: Short-to-medium-range jet airliner.

Power Plant: Four 6,700 lb st (29,8 kN) Textron Lycoming ALF 502R-3 or 6,970 lb st (31,0 kN) ALF 502R-5 or 7,000 lb st (31,1 kN) LF 507 turbofans.

Performance (-200): Max cruising speed, 423 kts (783 km/h) at 24,000 ft (7 315 m); economical cruise, 381 kts (706 km/h); range with max payload, 1,176 naut mls (2 179 km).

Accommodation: Flight crew of two. Typical one-class seating for (-100) up to 82 six-abreast or 70 five-abreast at 33-in (84-cm) seat pitch, or (-200) 96 passengers five-abreast or 112 six-abreast, at 29-in (74-cm) seat pitch.

Status: BAe 146-100 development aircraft flown 3 September 1981, 25 January 1982 and 2 April 1982. Certification, 7 February 1983, first delivery (to Dan-Air) 23 May 1983. First 146-200 flown on 1 August 1982. Certification 4 February 1983 and first service (Air Wisconsin) 27 June 1983. First -200QT Quiet Trader conversion entered service (TNT) 5 May 1987. First -200QC convertible flown May 1989.

Sales: Total sales of 207 by early 1991 (plus 86 options) included 29 Srs 100s, some for quasi-military use in VIP role. (See next entry also.)

Notes: The BAe 146 was designed (as the HS.146) at Hatfield by Hawker Siddeley Aviation prior to latter's nationalization as part of British Aerospace, which launched production of the 146 in July 1978. Production is spread throughout BAe factories in the UK with final assembly at Hatfield; Textron Aerostructures in USA and Saab-Scania in Sweden are producing wings and tail units respectively. Initial BAe 146-100 was followed by the -200 and -300 (see following entry) with successively lengthened fuselages. QC (quick-change) and QT ('Quiet Trader') freighter versions of the -100 and -200 are available. In 1990, BAe offered optimized regional jet transports as the RJ70 and RJ80 (with 70 or 80 seats respectively in standard -100 fuselage), with specialized new features. *Photo:* BAe 146-100 as RJ70 demonstrator.

BRITISH AEROSPACE 146-100 and -200

Dimensions: Span, 86 ft 5 in (26,34 m); overall length, (-100) 85 ft 11½ in (26,20 m); (-200) 93 ft 10 in (28,60 m); overall height, 28 ft 3 in (8,61 m); wing area, 832 sq ft (77,30 m²).

Weights (-200): Typical operating weight empty, 51,294 lb (23 266 kg); max payload, 23,700 lb (10 750 kg); max usable fuel, 2,704 lb (10 298 kg); max take-off, 93,000 lb (42 184 kg); max landing, 81,000 lb (36 741 kg); max zero fuel, 75,000 lb (34 019 kg).

BRITISH AEROSPACE 146-300

Dimensions: Span, 86 ft 5 in (26,34 m); overall length, 101 ft 8 in (30,99 m); overall height, 28 ft 2 in (8,60 m); wing area, 832 sq ft (77,3 m²).

Weights: Operating weight empty, 54,000 lb (24 494 kg); max payload, 24,549 lb (11 135 kg); max fuel, 22,704 lb (10 298 kg); max take-off, 97,500 lb (44 225 kg); max landing, 84,500 lb (38 328 kg); max zero fuel, 78,500 lb (35 607 kg).

BRITISH AEROSPACE 146-300

Country of Origin: United Kingdom.

Type: Short-to-medium-range jet airliner.

Power Plant: Four 6,970 lb st (31,0 kN) Textron Lycoming ALF 502R-5 or 7,000 lb st (31,1 kN) LF 507 turbofans.

Performance: Max cruising speed, 426 kts (789 km/h) at 29,000 ft (8 840 m); long-range cruise, 377 kts (699 km/h) at 29,000 ft (8 840 m); range with max payload, 1,090 naut mls (2 020 km); range with max fuel, 1,520 naut mls (2 817 km).

Accommodation: Flight crew of two. Typical arrangement for 103 passengers five-abreast. Maximum seating for 112 or (with suitable emergency exits) 122 five-abreast at 31-in (79-cm) seat pitch.

Status: Converted Srs 100 flown as aerodynamic prototype 1 May 1987. First production Srs 300 flown June 1988, certificated 6 September 1988, and entered service (Air Wisconsin) early 1989.

Sales: Orders for -300s total 48 for 10 operators.

Notes: The -300 is the second 'stretch' of the basic 146 Srs 100 (see previous entry) with a further 7 ft 10 in (2,37 m) extra length, the same as distinguishes the Srs 200 from the Srs 100. This allows the -300 to provide the same passenger capacity at five-abreast seating as the -200 in its six-abreast layout. QT Quiet Trader and QC Convertible versions are available and the TNT fleet for overnight freight services includes 10 Srs 300QTs so far. Introduction of LF 507 engines marked appearance of new standard of aircraft in 1991 with 4,000 lb (1 815 kg) increase in gross weight, greater payload and 150 naut mls (278 km) more range with max payload.

BRITISH AEROSPACE HS.748

Country of Origin: United Kingdom.
Type: Regional airliner.
Power Plant (Srs 2B): Two 2,280 ehp (1 982 kW) Rolls-Royce Dart RDa 7 Mk 552 turboprops.
Performance (Srs 2B): Typical cruising speed, 245 kts (454 km/h); max payload range, 1,007 naut mls (1 865 km) at cost economical cruise; max fuel range, 1,650 naut mls (3 055 km).
Accommodation: Normal flight crew of two and 48–52 passengers at 30-in (76-cm) pitch, four-abreast with central aisle.
Status: Two Avro 748 prototypes flown 24 June 1960 and 10 April 1961. First production Srs 1 flown 30 August 1961, certificated 7 December 1961, entered service with Skyways. Prototype Srs 2 flown 6 November 1961; certificated October 1962, entered service with BKS Air Transport. Prototype Srs 2C flown 31 December 1971. First production Srs 2B flown 22 June 1977. Super 748 first flown 30 July 1984.
Sales: Total of 18 Srs 1s built. Overall 748 sales total (military and civil), 382 by end 1988, when production ended, including 89 assembled by HAL in India. About 160 in service, early 1991.
Notes: The 748 provided steady business for what was the Avro company, now Manchester facilities of British Aerospace, since it entered production early in 1962. The Srs 1 had less powerful Dart engines and lower weights; Srs 2 and 2A differ in engine variants, Srs 2C has a large cargo loading door and Srs 2B has increased wing span and numerous product improvements. Introduced in 1983, the 748-2B Super has an advanced flight deck and engine hush-kits. *Photo:* HS.748 Srs 2A.

BRITISH AEROSPACE HS.748

Dimensions: Span, 102 ft 6 in (31,23 m); length, 67 ft 0 in (20,42 m); height, 24 ft 10 in (7,57 m); wing area, 828.87 sq ft (77,00 m²).
Weights (Srs 2B): Typical operational empty, 26,814 lb (12 163 kg); max payload, 11,686 lb (5 300 kg); max fuel, 11,520 lb (5 225 kg); max zero fuel, 38,500 lb (17 464 kg); max take-off, 46,500 lb (21 092 kg); max landing, 43,000 lb (19 505 kg).

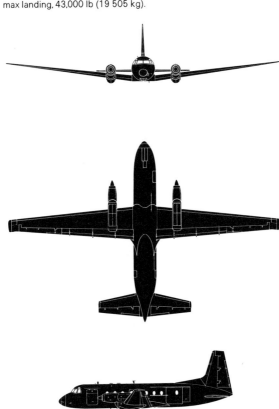

BRITISH AEROSPACE ATP

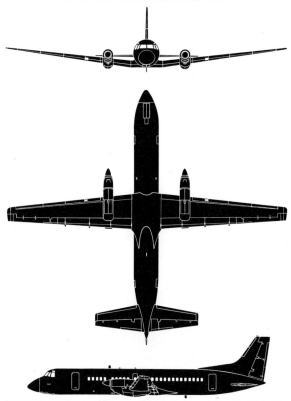

Dimensions: Span, 100 ft 6 in (30,63 m); overall length, 85 ft 4 in (26,00 m); overall height, 23 ft 5 in (7,14 m); wing area, 843 sq ft (78,30 m²).

Weights: Operating weight empty, 31,390 lb (14 238 kg); max payload, 15,510 lb (7 035 kg); max fuel, 11,200 lb (5 080 kg); max take-off, 50,550 lb (22 930 kg); max landing, 49,050 lb (22 250 kg); max zero fuel, 46,800 lb (21 228 kg).

BRITISH AEROSPACE ATP

Country of Origin: United Kingdom.

Type: Short-range regional airliner.

Power Plant: Two 2,230 shp (1 663 kW) Pratt & Whitney Canada PW124A or 2,182 shp (1 627 kW) PW126 or 2,388 shp (1 781 kW) PW126A turboprops.

Performance: Max cruising speed, 266 kts (493 km/h) at 13,000 ft (3 960 m); economical cruise, 236 kts (437 km/h) at 18,000 ft (5 485 m); range with max payload, 575 naut mls (1 065 km); range with max fuel, 1,860 naut mls (3 444 km).

Accommodation: Flight crew of two. Typical layout for 64 passengers, four-abreast. Max seating for 72, four-abreast at 30-in (76-cm) seat pitch.

Status: Marketing launch in September 1982 followed by full-scale development launch on 1 March 1984. First flight of initial test aircraft on 6 August 1986 and second on 20 February 1987. Certification (to JAR 25) in March 1988. Entry into service with British Midland on 9 May 1988.

Sales: Total of 39 ordered (early 1991) by Air Wisconsin, Airlines of Britain (British Midland, Loganair and Manx), Bangladesh Biman, British Airways, LAR and SATA.

Notes: The ATP (Advanced Turboprop) airliner is a product of the Manchester facilities of British Aerospace, being a derivative of the HS.748. It has the same fuselage cross-section but is about 18 ft (5,49 m) longer to accommodate four more seat rows. The wing structure is basically the same, with revised wingtips, and the vertical tail has slight sweepback. New engines have six-bladed propellers and an advanced technology flight deck is incorporated. PW126A engines became standard in 1990, together with rudder changes to improve control speeds, and new take-off flap settings.

BRITISH AEROSPACE JETSTREAM 31

Country of Origin: United Kingdom.
Type: Commuter liner and business twin.
Power Plant: Two 940 shp (701 kW) Garrett TPE331-10UF turbo-props.
Performance: Max cruising speed, 263 kts (488 km/h) at 15,000 ft (4 570 m); best economy cruising speed, 230 kts (426 km/h) at 25,000 ft (7 620 m); range with 18 passengers, 675 naut mls (1 250 km); range with nine passengers, 1,065 naut mls (1 975 km).
Accommodation: Flight crew of two and up to 19 passengers three-abreast with off-set aisle at 30/31-in (76/79-cm) pitch.
Status: Prototype (derived from original Handley Page production variant) first flown on 28 March 1980. First two production Jetstream 31s flown on 18 March and 26 May 1982 respectively. British certification 29 June 1982 and US certification 30 November 1982. Production deliveries commenced 15 and 30 December 1982 (to Contactair and Peregrine respectively). Super 31 certificated 7 October 1988.
Sales: Total of 220 Jetstream 31s and 125 Super Jetstream 31s sold by early 1991.
Notes: Jetstream 31 is the re-launched BAe production version of original HP.137 offered in 18/19-seat commuter, 12-seat executive shuttle and nine-seat corporate versions. The commuter version has proved to be the best seller to date, and has sold particularly well in the US where it is used by several airlines flying services in and out of the major hubs. In 1987, the Super 31, now the sole production version alongside the Jetstream 41 (see next entry), has uprated TPE331-12 engines, higher weights and improved performances as quoted above.

BRITISH AEROSPACE JETSTREAM 31

Dimensions: Span, 52 ft 0 in (15,85 m); length, 47 ft 1½ in (14,37 m); height, 17 ft 6 in (5,37 m); wing area, 271.3 sq ft (25,20 m²).
Weights: Operational weight empty, 9,570 lb (4 341 kg); max payload, 3,980 lb (1 805 kg); max fuel weight, 3,024 lb (1 372 kg); max take-off, 15,212 lb (6 900 kg); max landing weight, 14,550 lb (6 600 kg).

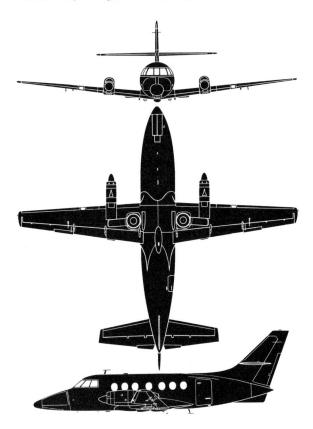

BRITISH AEROSPACE JETSTREAM 41

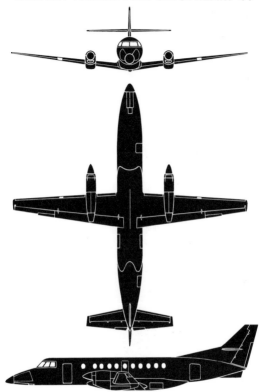

Dimensions: Span, 60 ft 0 in (18,29 m); overall length, 63 ft 2 in (19,25 m); overall height, 18 ft 10 in (5,74 m); wing area, 350 sq ft (32,50 m²).

Weights: Operating weight empty, 13,544 lb (6 144 kg); max payload, 6,298 lb (82 856 kg); max fuel 5,760 lb (2 613 kg); max take-off, 22,377 lb (10 150 kg); max landing, 21,715 lb (9 850 kg); max zero fuel, 19,842 lb (9 000 kg).

BRITISH AEROSPACE JETSTREAM 41

Country of Origin: United Kingdom.
Type: Commuter and regional airliner.
Power Plant: Two 1,500 shp (1 120 kW) Garrett TPE331-14GR/HR turboprops.
Performance: Max cruising speed, 292 kts (537 km/h) at 20,000 ft (6 100 m); economical cruise, 260 kts (481 km/h) at 29,000 ft (8 870 m); range with max payload, 590 naut mls (1 093 km).
Accommodation: Flight crew of two. Standard seating for 29, three-abreast at 30-in (76-cm) seat pitch.
Status: Launch announced on 24 May 1989, to achieve first flight in mid-1991 and service entry in the autumn of 1992.
Sales: Launch order for 10 confirmed in March 1990 by Pan Am Express. Options on 50 held by American Eagle.
Notes: Jetstream 41 differs from Super 31 (previous entry) in having a lengthened fuselage with improved cabin access, and wing 'lowered', relative to fuselage, to eliminate the step in the cabin floor. The span is increased to match the higher weights at which the Jetstream 41 operates. Many systems improvements have been made. Risk-sharing partners in the Jetstream 41 are Pilatus (Switzerland) and Field Aircraft Ltd. Wing production is by Gulfstream Aerospace at Savannah, Ga.

BRITISH AEROSPACE (BAC) ONE-ELEVEN

Country of Origin: United Kingdom.
Type: Short-range jet transport.
Power Plant (Srs 500): Two 12,550 lb st (55,8 kN) Rolls-Royce Spey 512 DW or (Srs 2000/2400) 15,100 lb st (67,2 kN) Rolls-Royce Tay 650 turbofans.
Performance: (Srs 500): Max cruise, 470 kts (870 km/h) at 21,000 ft (6 400 km); best economy cruise, 400 kts (742 km/h) at 25,000 ft (7 620 m); range with typical max payload, 1,480 naut mls (2 744 km); max range, 1,880 naut mls (3,484 km).
Accommodation: Flight crew of two and up to 119 passengers five-abreast, with off-set aisle, at 29-in (74-cm) pitch.
Status: Prototype first flown 20 August 1963; first production Srs 200 flown 19 December 1963, certification 6 April 1965 followed by first services on 9 April (BUA) and 25 April (Braniff). Prototype Srs 300/400 flown 13 July 1965; Srs 400 certification 22 November 1965. Prototype Srs 500 flown 30 June 1967 and first production Srs 500 on 7 February 1968 and certificated 18 August 1968. Prototype Srs 475 flown 27 August 1970 and first production on 5 April 1971, with certification in July. Production in UK complete. First Srs 560 flown in Romania 18 September 1982. First Srs 2400 (Tays) flown in US 2 July 1990.
Sales: Total of 232 built in UK including 56 Srs 200, nine Srs 300, 69 Srs 400, nine Srs 475 and 89 Srs 500.
Notes: One-Eleven Srs 200, 300 and 400 are dimensionally similar; Srs 500 has longer fuselage and extended wing tips and Srs 475 has original fuselage with extended wing and uprated engines. Following delivery of last One-Eleven in mid-1982, British Aerospace supplied components for 22 more to be assembled in Romania, of which 10 were completed by 1987. CNIAR is now working on Tay-engined variants (Srs 2000) for delivery from 1991. Dee Howard in the US completed the first One-Eleven 2400 with Tays and was proceeding with certification in 1991. *Photo:* BAC One-Eleven 2400.

BRITISH AEROSPACE (BAC) ONE-ELEVEN

Dimensions (Srs 500): Span, 93 ft 6 in (28,50 m); length, 107 ft 0 in (32,61 m); height, 24 ft 6 in (7,47 m); wing area, 1,031 sq ft (95,78 m²).
Weights (Srs 500): Typical operating empty, 54,582 lb (24 758 kg); max payload, 26,418 lb (11 983 kg); max zero fuel, 81,000 lb (36 741 kg); max take-off, 104,500 lb (47 400 kg); max landing, 87,000 lb (39 463 kg).

CANADAIR CL-601 REGIONAL JET

Dimensions: Span, 70 ft 4 in (21,44 m); overall length, 88 ft 5 in (26,95 m); overall height, 20 ft 8 in (6,30 m); gross wing area, 581.1 sq ft (53,99 m²).

Weights: Operating weight empty, 30,100 lb (13 653 kg); max fuel, 9,380 lb (4 255 kg); max payload, 12,100 lb (5 488 kg); max take-off, 47,450 lb (21 523 kg); max landing, 44,700 lb (20 276 kg); max zero fuel, 42,200 lb (19 142 kg).

CANADAIR CL-601 REGIONAL JET

Country of Origin: Canada.
Type: Regional jet transport.
Power Plant: Two General Electric CF34-3A turbofans each rated at 9,220 lb st (41,0 kN) for take-off, with APR.
Performance: Max cruise, 459 kts (851 km/h) at 36,000 ft (11 000 m); economical cruise, 424 kts (786 km/h) at 36,000 ft (11 000 m); max operating altitude, 41,000 ft (12 500 m); range with 50-passenger payload, 845–1,418 naut mls (1 564–2 626 km).
Accommodation: Flight crew of two. Standard layout provides 50 seats, four-abreast, at a pitch of 31 in (79 cm). Maximum high-density layout, 56 passengers.
Status: Launched formally in March 1989 after completion of a one-year advanced design phase. First flight scheduled for mid-1991, for deliveries to start in second quarter of 1992. Planned production rate, four per month.
Sales: Orders and option commitments for 119 announced, for eight customers in six countries. Launch customer, DLT, ordered 13 Srs 100ER, with 12 on option.
Notes: The RJ is a stretched derivative of the Challenger 601-3A corporate jet transport, with the fuselage lengthened by 20 ft (6,1 m), an increase in wing area of some 15 per cent, and many systems improvements. Data above are for Srs 100. The Srs 100ER has higher gross weight of 51,000 lb (23 133 kg) and more fuel for a range of 1,476 naut mls (2 736 km). The Srs 200 is projected as a follow-on with fuselage stretched for 70–74 seats, and more powerful engines.

CASA C-212 AVIOCAR

Country of Origin: Spain.
Type: Light twin-turboprop regional transport.
Power Plant: Two Garrett TPE331-10R-513C turboprops each flat-rated at 900 shp (671 kW) for take-off, and at 925 shp (690 kW) with APR.
Performance: Max cruising speed, 191 kts (354 km/h) at 10,000 ft (3 050 m); economical cruise, 162 kts (300 km/h) at 10,000 ft (3 050 m); range with max payload, 237 naut mls (440 km); range with max fuel, 773 naut mls (1 433 km).
Accommodation: Flight crew of two. Typical layout for 22 passengers, three-abreast. Max seating for 26, three-abreast at 28.5-in (72-cm) seat pitch.
Status: Prototype C-212 flown 26 March 1971; 138th and 139th production aircraft became prototypes for the Srs 200, the first of these flying on 30 April 1978. Deliveries of Srs 200 commenced early 1980. Srs 300 first flown 1984, certificated December 1987.
Sales: More than 450 sold, from production in Spain and Indonesia, of which nearly half for civil use. Total includes 135 Srs 100 by CASA plus 29 by IPTN.
Notes: CASA developed the C-212 primarily for military use and later achieved useful commercial sales, helped by licence-production in Indonesia (as the NC-212). The original Srs 100 had lower-rated TPE331-5 engines and lower weights; Srs 200 had TPE331-10s and both have fuselage incorporating rear loading ramp and original 62 ft 4 in (19,00 m) span without winglets. Data and photo are for Srs 300.

CASA C-212 AVIOCAR

Dimensions: Span 66 ft 6½ in (20,28 m); overall length, 52 ft 11¾ in (16,15 m); overall height, 21 ft 7¾ in (6,60 m); wing area, 441.3 sq ft (41,0 m²).

Weights (Srs 300): Operational weight empty, 10,053 lb (4 560 kg); max cargo payload, 5,952 lb (2 700 kg); max fuel, 3,527 lb (1 600 kg); max take-off, 16,975 lb (7 700 kg); max landing, 16,424 lb (7 450 kg); max zero fuel, 15,653 lb (7 100 kg).

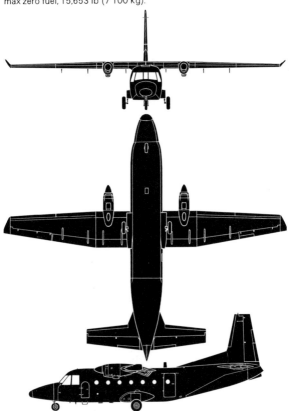

CONVAIR 580 (and 600, 640)

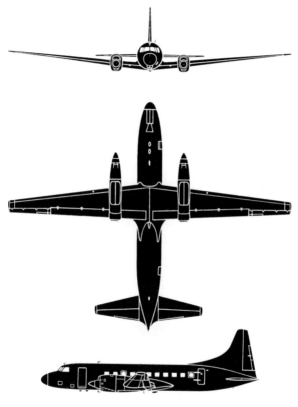

Dimensions: Span, 105 ft 4 in (32,12 m); length, 81 ft 6 in (24,84 m); height, 29 ft 2 in (8,89 m); wing area, 920 sq ft (85,5 m²).
Weights: Operating weight empty, 30,275 lb (13 732 kg); max payload, 8,870 lb (4 023 kg); max fuel, 13,887 lb (6 299 kg); max take-off, 58,140 lb (26 371 kg); max landing, 52,000 lb (23 187 kg).

CONVAIR 580

Country of Origin: USA.

Type: Short-range turboprop airliner.

Power Plant: Two, 3,750 shp (2 800 kW) Allison 501-D13H turboprops.

Performance: Max cruise, 297 kts (550 km/h) at 20,000 ft (6 100 m), range with 5,000-lb (2 270-kg) payload, 1,970 naut mls (3 650 km); range with max fuel, 2,577 naut mls (4 773 km).

Accommodation: Flight crew of two or three, and up to 56 passengers four-abreast with central aisle, at 30-in (76-cm) pitch.

Status: CV-240 Turboliner prototype flown 29 December 1950 and YC-131C conversion with Allison 501D turboprops flown 29 June 1954; first CV-580 Allison-Convair flown 19 January 1960, certificated 21 April 1960 and entered airline service (Frontier) June 1964. Eland-Convair conversion flown 9 February 1955, entered airline service (Allegheny) July 1959. CV-600 (Dart engines) first flown 20 May 1965, certificated 18 November, entered service (Central Airlines) 30 November 1965; CV-640 first flown 20 August 1965, certificated 7 December 1965, entered service (Caribair) 22 December 1965. Super 580 prototype flown 21 March 1984.

Sales: Total of 170 CV-340s/440s converted to CV-580 of which 110 for airline use. Total of 38 CV-240s converted to CV-600 and 27 CV-340s/440s to CV-640s, for airline use. About 75 CV-580s and 35 CV-600/640s in airline service in 1990.

Notes: Several schemes for converting piston-engined airliners to have turboprop engines were projected during the 'fifties, but only the Convair 240/340/440 family was adopted for such conversion on a large scale. In 1984, Allison sponsored development of the Super 580 with uprated 501-D22G engines and projected a stretched-fuselage derivative as the Allison Flagship. *Photo:* Convair 580.

DASSAULT-BREGUET MERCURE

Country of Origin: France.
Type: Short-range jet transport.
Power Plant: Two 15,500 lb st (69 kN) Pratt & Whitney JT8D-15 turbofans.
Performance: Max cruise, 500 kts (926 km/h) at 20,000 ft (6 100 m); best economy cruise, 463 kts (858 km/h) at 30,000 ft (9 145 m); range with max payload, 600 naut mls (1 110 km); range with max fuel, 1,750 naut mls (3 240 km).
Accommodation: Flight crew of two; typical mixed-class seating. 12F four-abreast at 38-in (96,5-cm) pitch and 108 E six-abreast at 32-in (81,5-cm) pitch; maximum passenger capacity 162 at 30-in (76-cm) pitch.
Status: Two prototypes flown 28 May 1971 and 7 September 1972. First production aircraft flown 17 July 1973, certificated 12 February 1974, entered service (Air Inter) 4 June 1974. Certificated for Cat III operation 30 September 1974. Production completed.
Sales: Ten aircraft ordered by Air Inter 29 January 1972, all still in service together with updated second prototype; no other sales were made.
Notes: The Mercure was intended by Dassault to provide a basis for the company to expand its commercial activities and was put into production with only one airline order, placed by the French domestic operator Air Inter. Consequently, considerable losses were made on the programme by Dassault and the French government, as well as risk-sharing partners in Italy, Spain, Belgium, Switzerland and Canada. An attempt to launch a developed Mercure 200 with McDonnell Douglas participation did not succeed.

DASSAULT-BREGUET MERCURE

Dimensions: Span, 100 ft 3 in (30,55 m); length, 114 ft 3½ in (34,84 m); height 37 ft 3¼ in (11,36 m); wing area, 1,249 sq ft (116,0 m²).

Weights: Operating weight empty, 70,107 lb (31 800 kg); max fuel load, 32,520 lb (14 750 kg); max payload, 35,715 lb (16 200 kg); max zero fuel, 105,820 lb (48 000 kg); max take-off, 124,560 lb (56 500 kg); max landing, 114,640 lb (52 000 kg).

DE HAVILLAND CANADA TWIN OTTER

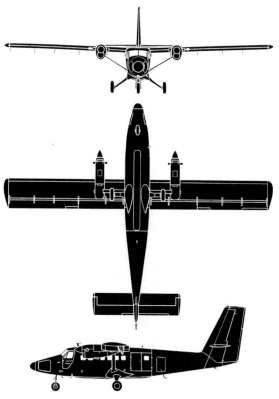

Dimensions: Span, 65 ft 0 in (19,81 m); length, 51 ft 9 in (15,77 m); height, 19 ft 6 in (5,94 m); wing area, 420 sq ft (39,02 m²).
Weights: Operating weight empty, 7,415 lb (3 363 kg); max payload, 4,280 lb (1 941 kg); max fuel load, 2,583 lb (1 171 kg); max zero fuel, 12,300 lb (5 579 kg); max take-off, 12,500 lb (5 670 kg); max landing, 12,300 lb (5 579 kg).

DE HAVILLAND CANADA TWIN OTTER

Country of Origin: Canada.

Type: Commuter and light transport.

Power Plant: Two 652 shp (487 kW) Pratt & Whitney PT6A-27 turboprops.

Performance: Max cruise, 182 kts (337 km/h) at 10,000 ft (3 050 m); long-range cruise, 145 kts (269 km/h) at 10,000 ft (3 050 m); range with 2,500-lb (1 134-kg) payload, 700 naut mls (1 297 km).

Accommodation: Flight crew of one or two and up to 20 passengers seated at 30-in (76-cm) pitch three-abreast.

Status: Prototype first flown 20 May 1965; certification May 1966; initial deliveries July 1966. First deliveries of Srs 200, April 1968 and Srs 300, Spring 1969.

Sales: Total 844 sold by late 1988 (including military and non-airline commercial sales) when production ended. First 115 aircraft were Series 100, next 115 were Series 200, thereafter Series 300.

Notes: As its name suggests, the DHC-6 Twin Otter began life as a twin-engined derivative of the single piston-engined Otter, with which it shares some wing and fuselage components. It proved to have excellent appeal in the commuter and third-level airline market, with its STOL performance allowing it to bring reliable scheduled service to many close-in town airports. Original Series 100 had shorter nose and Series 300 introduced the uprated PT6A-27 engines. Floatplane, skiplane and amphibious versions are available, and de Havilland developed a Srs 300M Twin Otter for more specifically military rôles, with wing strong points and provision for a search radar under the nose. This version, and some Srs 300s in civilian but non-airline use, operate at a higher gross weight. *Photo:* Srs 300.

DE HAVILLAND CANADA DASH 7

Country of Origin: Canada.
Type: STOL regional airliner.
Power Plant: Four 1,120 shp (835 kW) Pratt & Whitney PT6A-50 turboprops.
Performance: Max cruise, 227 kts (420 km/h) at 15,000 ft (4 575 m); long-range cruise, 215 kts (399 km/h) at 20,000 ft (6 100 m); range (with 50-passenger payload), 690 naut mls (1 279 km); max range, 1,170 naut mls (2 168 km).
Accommodation: Flight crew of two and up to 54 passengers at 29-in (74-cm) pitch four-abreast with central aisle.
Status: Two prototypes first flown 27 March and 26 June 1975 respectively. First production aircraft flown 30 May 1977, entered service 3 February 1978 (with Rocky Mountain Airways). Delivery of Srs 150 began in 1986.
Sales: Total of 111 built, production ended in 1988.
Notes: Dash-7 was the largest of the DH Canada family of quiet STOL airliners, production ending after Boeing acquired the company in 1986. Basic Srs 100 is described above. Other variants were Series 101 in all cargo configuration, DHC-7R Ranger specially equipped for the Canadian Coast Guard, and the Srs 150 (and 151 freighter) with gross weight of 47,000 lb (21 319 kg) and provision for extra 912 Imp gal (4 154 l) of fuel in wing tanks, increasing range to 2,525 naut mls (4 679 km).

DE HAVILLAND CANADA DASH 7

Dimensions: Span, 93 ft 0 in (28,35 m); length, 80 ft 6 in (24,54 m); height, 26 ft 2 in (7,98 m); wing area, 860 sq ft (79,9 m²).
Weights: Operating weight empty, 27,690 lb (12 560 kg); max fuel, 10,060 lb (4 563 kg); max payload, 11,306 lb (5 127 kg); max zero fuel, 39,000 lb (17 690 kg); max take-off, 44,000 lb (19 958 kg); max landing, 44,000 lb (19 958 kg).

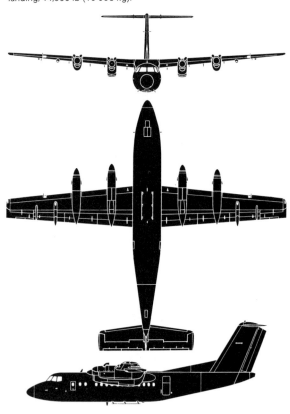

DE HAVILLAND CANADA DASH 8 SRS 100

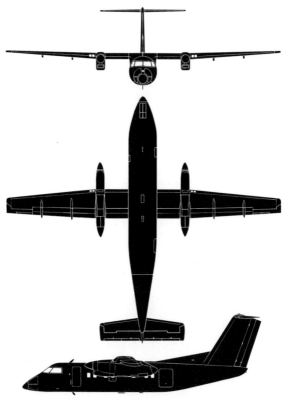

Dimensions: Span, 85 ft 0 in (25,91 m); length, 73 ft 0 in (22,25 m); height, 24 ft 7 in (7,49 m); wing area, 585 sq ft (54,30 m²).

Weights: Operating weight empty, 21,590 lb (9 793 kg); standard fuel weight, 5,678 lb (2 576 kg); max payload, 7,824 lb (3 549 kg); max zero fuel, 31,000 lb (14 062 kg); max take-off, 34,500 lb (15 649 kg); max landing, 33,900 lb (14 923 kg).

DE HAVILLAND CANADA DASH 8 SRS 100

Country of Origin: Canada.

Type: Short-range regional airliner.

Power Plant: Two 2,000 shp (1 491 kW) Pratt & Whitney PW120A or 2,150 shp (1 679 kW) PW121 turboprops.

Performance: Max cruise, 265 kts (554 km/h) at 25,000 ft (7 620 m); long-range cruise, 237 kts (439 km/h); range with max payload (36 passengers), 1,150 naut mls (2 130 km).

Accommodation: Flight crew of two and 36 passengers at 31-in (79-cm) pitch four-abreast with central aisle; maximum, 40.

Status: First of four pre-production aircraft flown 20 June 1983, second on 26 October 1983. Canadian certification on 28 September 1984. First delivery (norOntair) 23 October 1984.

Sales: Total Dash 8 sales including options, 351 by end-1990, of which 246 for the Srs 100.

Notes: The Dash 8 (DHC-8) was designed to serve as a junior partner with the Dash 7, with which it shares a similar configuration, featuring a high wing and T-tail. Like the larger aircraft, the Dash 8 depends upon large-area trailing edge flaps and a sophisticated control system for its low-speed performance and control, without the use of leading-edge flaps. Intended primarily for use by the regional airlines, the Dash 8 is also offered with mixed passenger/cargo layouts including quick-change options. The Srs 101 was initial production version with PW120 engines, Srs 102 has PW120As and higher weights, and Srs 103 has PW121s for high-temperature operations. Srs 100A, introduced in 1990, featured an improved interior.

DE HAVILLAND CANADA DASH 8 SRS 300

Country of Origin: Canada.

Type: Short-range regional airliner.

Power Plant: Two 2,380 shp (1 776 kW) Pratt & Whitney PW123 turboprops.

Performance: Max cruising speed, 285 kts (528 km/h) at 15,000 ft (4 570 m); range with 50-passenger payload, 800 naut mls (1 482 km); range (Srs 300A high gross weight option), 1,250 naut mls (2 315 km); range with max fuel, 2,050 naut mls (3 800 km).

Accommodation: Flight crew of two and up to 56 passengers four-abreast with single aisle at 29-in (74-cm) pitch; typical layout for 50 passengers at 32-in (81-cm) pitch.

Status: Full-scale development confirmed during 1986, with modification of a Srs 100 to serve as the first prototype, for first flight on 15 May 1987. Two additional aircraft for flight development flew later in 1987. Canadian certification 14 February and US certification 8 June 1989. First delivery (Time Air) 27 February 1989. First delivery, high gross weight version (Contact Air) 24 August 1990.

Sales: Total of 105 by early 1991.

Notes: The successful entry into service of the Dash 8 Srs 100 (see previous pages) in 1985 led de Havilland to study a number of possible derivative models. These included an increased gross weight option for the Srs 100 itself, as well as corporate and military variants; in addition, a possible stretch of the basic aircraft began to be seriously studied. Although the 50/56-seat Dash 7 was already in production, a Dash 8 enlarged to similar capacity offered more attractive economics, since it used only two engines. Following the acquisition of de Havilland by Boeing early in 1986, whereupon it became a subsidiary of Boeing Canada Ltd, the basic Srs 301 was joined by the Srs 320B with higher weights (marketed in 1990 as the Srs 300A, with an improved interior) and the Srs 320C Combi.

DE HAVILLAND CANADA DASH 8 SRS 300

Dimensions: Span, 90 ft 0 in (27,43 m); length, 84 ft 3 in (25,68 m); height, 24 ft 7 in (7,49 m); wing area, 605 sq ft (56,20 m²).

Weights: Operating weight empty, 25,700 lb (11 657 kg); max payload, 11,500 lb (5 216 kg); max fuel, 5,678 lb (2 576 kg); max take-off, 41,100–43,000 lb (18 642–19 505 kg); max landing, 40,000 lb (18 145 kg); max zero fuel, 37,200 lb (16 873 kg).

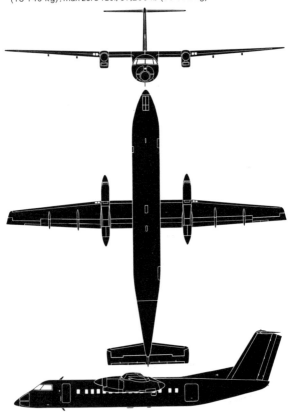

DORNIER (DEUTSCHE AEROSPACE) 228-200

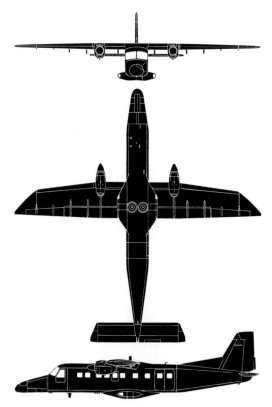

Dimensions: Span, 55 ft 8 in (16,97 m); overall length, 54 ft 3 in (16,55 m); overall height, 75 ft 11¼ in (4,86 m); wing area, 344.5 sq ft (32,0 m²).
Weights: Operating weight empty, 8,153 lb (3 698 kg); max payload, 4,178 lb (1 895 kg); max take-off, 13,668 lb (6 200 kg); max landing, 13,007 lb (5 900 kg); max zero fuel, 11,900 lb (5 400 kg).

DORNIER (DEUTSCH AEROSPACE) 228-200

Country of Origin: Germany.

Type: Commuter and light transport.

Power Plant: Two Garrett TPE 331-5-252D turboprops each rated at 776 shp (579 kW) for take-off.

Performance: Max cruising speed, 231 kts (428 km/h) at 10,000 ft (3 050 m); economical cruise, 180 kts (333 km/h); range with max payload, 540 naut mls (1 000 km); range with max fuel, 1,640 naut mls (3 040 km).

Accommodation: Flight crew of one or two. Typical layout for 19 passengers, two-abreast at 30-in (76-cm) seat pitch.

Status: The prototypes of the Do 228-100 and -200 flew respectively on 28 March and 9 May 1981, and were certificated on 18 December 1981 and 6 September 1982 respectively. Deliveries of the Srs 100 (to A/S Norving) began in February 1982. Model 228-212 certificated April 1989. First flight of Indian-assembled example on 31 January 1986 and deliveries from the Hindustan Aeronautics assembly line at Kanpur (to Vayudoot) began 22 March 1986.

Sales: Total sales at November 1990, 191 in all versions, plus Indian production of up to 150.

Notes: The Srs 100 and Srs 200 differ only in fuselage length, the former being the short-fuselage version with 15 seats. Principal production version, starting with production number 176, is the 228-212, which has higher take-off and landing weights of 14,110 lb (6 400 kg) and 13,448 lb (6 100 kg) respectively. Several specialized military variants have also been developed.

DORNIER (DEUTSCHE AEROSPACE) 328

Country of Origin: Germany.

Type: Regional turboprop transport.

Power Plant: Two Pratt & Whitney Canada PW119 turboprops each rated at 2,180 shp (1 627 kW) for take-off.

Performance: Max cruising speed, 345 kts (640 km/h); range with max payload, 700 naut mls (1 300 km); range with 16 passengers, 1,500 naut mls (1 300 km); range with 16 passengers, 1,500 naut mls (2 780 km).

Accommodation: Flight crew of two. Typical layout for 30 passengers, three-abreast. Max seating for 39, four-abreast at 30-in (76-cm) pitch.

Status: Programme launched in 1987 and progressing towards first flight summer 1991 and European certification in late 1992 for customer deliveries to begin early 1993. FAA certification first quarter 1993 for deliveries to first US customer, Midway Commuter.

Sales: Firm orders for 40 and 51 options at end of 1990, for seven customers including Contact Air (Germany), Sunshine Aviation (Switzerland), Midway Connection (US), Afrimex Aviation (Nigeria), Air Calédonie (New Caledonia), Cayenne Ltd (UK) and Tahiti Conquest Airlines (French Polynesia).

Notes: Dornier 328 was developed to provide a 'big brother' for the Model 228 (see previous entry), and against market studies indicating potential sales of some 400 aircraft up to year 2006. Basic aircraft is a 30-seater, three-abreast, but a high-density version features four-abreast seating and a stretched Dornier 328S to seat up to 50 is already in the planning stage, with a fuselage length of 89 ft 6 in (27,3 m).

DORNIER (DEUTSCHE AEROSPACE) 328

Dimensions: Span, 68 ft 10 in (20,98 m); overall length, 69 ft 8 in (21,22 m); overall height, 29 ft 8 in.

Weights: Max payload, 7,605 lb (3 450 kg); max take-off, 27,558 lb (12 500 kg); max landing, 27,006 lb (12 250 kg); max zero fuel, 25,628 lb (11 625 kg).

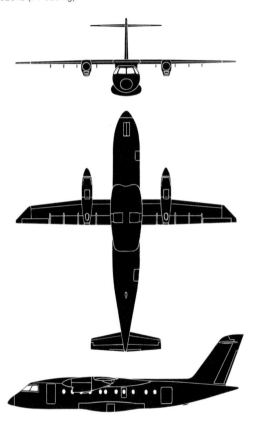

DOUGLAS DC-3

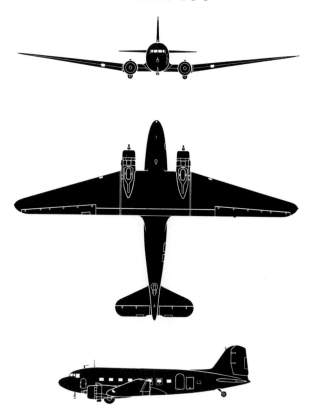

Dimensions: Span, 95 ft 0 in (28,96 m); length, 64 ft 6 in (19,66 m); height, 16 ft 11½ in (5,16 m); wing area, 987 sq ft (91,7 m²).
Weights: Typical operating weight empty, 17,720 lb (8 030 kg); max payload, 6,600 lb (2 994 kg); max fuel, 4,820 lb (2 186 kg); max take-off, 28,000 lb (12 700 kg); max landing, 26,900 lb (12 202 kg).

DOUGLAS DC-3

Country of Origin: USA.

Type: Short-range passenger and freight transport.

Power Plant: Two 1,200 hp (896 kW) Pratt & Whitney R-1830-92 Twin Wasp air-cooled radial engines.

Performance (Typical commercial operation, post-war): Max speed, 187 kts (346 km/h); economical cruise, 143 kts (266 km/h) at 6,000 ft (1 830 m); range with max payload, 305 naut mls (563 km); range with max fuel, 1,312 naut mls (2 430 km).

Accommodation: Flight crew of two; typical passenger layout provides for 28–32, four-abreast at up to 38-in (96.5-cm) pitch with central aisle.

Status: DST (prototype for DC-3 series) first flown 17 December 1935; first service use (American Airlines) 25 June 1936. Production completed 1946.

Sales: Total of 10,655 built, including 430 for commercial customers prior to December 1941, 10,197 for military use before and during World War II and 28 assembled post-war from surplus components as DC-3Ds. About 300 were still in airline service at the end of 1990.

Notes: The DC-3 established an outstanding reputation in the five years before the USA entered World War II, as the most efficient and comfortable short-medium-range airliner then available. Adopted for military use, it gained more fame as the C-47 Skytrain and the Dakota, and many thousands were civilianized after the war ended to provide the backbone of the air transport industry in the early post-war years. They have proved almost indestructible, and still play a part in the air transport system of many nations, especially in the Third World.

EMBRAER EMB-110 BANDEIRANTE

Country of Origin: Brazil.
Type: Regional airliner.
Power Plant: Two Pratt & Whitney Canada PT6A-34 turboprops each rated at 750 shp (559 kW) for take-off.
Performance: Max cruising speed, 222 kts (413 km/h) at 8,000 ft (2 440 m); economical cruise, 184 kts (341 km/h) at 10,000 ft (3 050 m); range with max fuel, 1,060 naut mls (1 964 km).
Accommodation: Flight crew of two. Typical layout for 18 passengers, three-abreast. Max seating for 21, three-abreast at 29-in (74-cm) seat pitch.
Status: Military prototypes first flown 26 October 1968, 19 October 1969 and 26 June 1970; first production EMB-110 flown 9 August 1972; first airline use (15-seat EMB-110C) 16 April 1973. Stretched EMB-110P2 first flown 3 May 1977. Production rate, approx six a month.
Sales: Total of 500 built, including military variants. Production now ended.
Notes: The unpressurized Bandeirante originated to a Brazilian military specification. EMB-110P2 is basic all-passenger (up to 21 seats) version, P1 has larger rear-loading door for passenger/cargo convertible operations. Original certification basis for the commercial Bandeirante was FAR-23 at 12,500 lb (5 670 kg) gross weight; the recertificated EMB-110/41 (to SFAR 41) operates at weights quoted here. Commencing with the 439th aircraft in 1983, a number of refinements were introduced, including dihedral on the tailplane, resulting in the designations EMB-110P1A, -110P1A/41, -110P2A and -110P2A/41.
Photo: EMB-110P1.

EMBRAER EMB-110 BANDEIRANTE

Dimensions: Span, 50 ft 3½ in (15,33 m); overall length, 49 ft 6½ in (15,10 m); overall height 16 ft 1¾ in (4,92 m); wing area, 313.2 sq ft (29,10 m²).
Weights: Operating weight empty, 7,915 lb (3 590 kg); max payload, 3,443 lb (1 561 kg); max fuel, 2,883 lb (1 308 kg); max take-off, 13,010 lb (5 900 kg); max landing, 12,566 lb (5 700 kg); max zero fuel, 12,015 lb (5 450 kg).

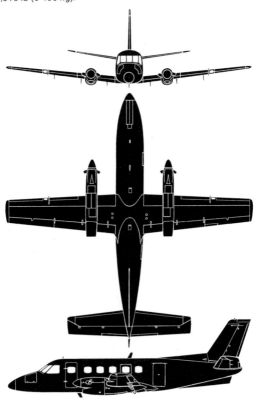

EMBRAER EMB-120 BRASILIA

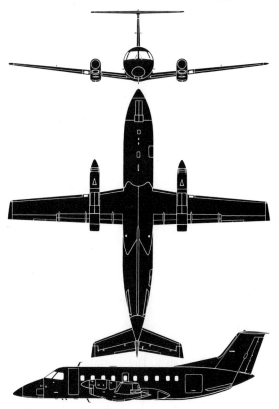

Dimensions: Span, 64 ft 10¾ in (19,78 m); length 65 ft 7 in (20,00 m); height, 20 ft 10 in (6,35 m); wing area, 424.46 sq ft (39,43 m²).
Weights: Operating weight empty, 15,586 lb (7 070 kg); max fuel, 5,862 lb (2 659 kg); max payload, 7,650 lb (3 470 kg); max zero fuel, 23,148 lb (10 500 kg); max take-off 25,353 lb (11 500 kg); max landing, 24,802 lb (11 250 kg).

EMBRAER EMB-120 BRASILIA

Country of Origin: Brazil.

Type: Regional airliner.

Power Plant: Two 1,800 shp (1 343 kW) Pratt & Whitney Canada PW118 turboprops.

Performance: Max cruise, 298 kts (552 km/h) at 22,000 ft (6 705 m); long-range cruise, 260 kts (482 km/h) at 25,000 ft (7 620 m); max payload range (30 passengers), 945 naut mls (1 750 km) at econ cruise; max fuel range, 1,610 naut mls (2 982 km).

Accommodation: Flight crew of two and 30 passengers at 31-in (79-cm) pitch three-abreast with offset aisle. Optional arrangements for 24 and 26 passengers with enlarged baggage compartment.

Status: First Brasilia entered flight test on 27 July 1983, second on 21 December and third on 9 May 1984. Certification in Brazil on 16 May 1985 and in USA on 9 July 1985. First production delivery (to ASA) August 1985.

Sales: Orders and options total 494 by February 1991, with 214 delivered.

Notes: Design work on the EMB-120 Brasilia was launched in September 1979, the structural design having been finalized in January 1982. Corporate transport and all-cargo versions are available and proposed versions include military models for maritime surveillance, aeromedical evacuation, electronic intelligence, paratroop transportation and search and rescue. Initial aircraft were powered by the 1,500 shp (1 120 kW) PW115 engines, a switch being made to the more powerful PW118 or 'hot and high' PW118A in 1986.

EMBRAER EMB-145

Country of Origin: Brazil.

Type: Regional jet airliner.

Power Plant: Two General Motors Allison GMA-3007 turbofans each flat rated at 6,750 lb st (30,03 kN) for take-off.

Performance: Max cruising speed, 392 kts (726 km/h) at 10,000 ft (3 050 m), 412 kts (763 km/h) at 20,000 ft (6 100 m), 431 kts (799 km/h) at 33,000 ft (10 060 m); range with max payload, 650 naut mls (1 205 km); range with 50 passengers, 930 naut mls (1 725 km).

Accommodation: Flight crew of two and one cabin attendant. Standard layouts provide 45, 48 or 50 seats, three-abreast with off-set 17-in (43-cm) aisle and at a pitch of 31 in (79 cm).

Status: Announced June 1989. Flight testing to begin in final quarter of 1991. Certification last quarter of 1992 with delivery of six aircraft by end of that year.

Sales: Total of 297 options and other commitments reported to be held by Embraer by May 1990, from operators in 13 countries. Largest options are for Comair (60), Northwest Airlink (45), Skywest (20) and Business Express (20).

Notes: The EMB-145 is basically a jet adaptation of the EMB-120 Brasilia turboprop twin, with which it has 75 per cent commonality. The fuselage has the same cross section but is longer, to provide better facilities (galleys, toilets, baggage stowage, etc) for the same number of passengers. The configuration, data and schedule shown here were for the EMB-145 as launched in mid-1989 but in 1990 Embraer was studying possible alternatives with less commonality with the EMB-145, perhaps with wing sweepback and underwing engine location. Final configuration and revised schedules were to be estabiished in 1991.

EMBRAER EMB-145

Dimensions: Span, 73 ft 9 in (22,49 m); overall length, 88 ft 10 in (27,08 m); overall height, 20 ft 8 in (6,31 m); wheelbase, 35 ft 10 in (10,92 m); undercarriage track, 21 ft 7 in (6,58 m); wing area, 538 sq ft (50,0 m²).

Weights: Basic operating, 24,118 lb (10 940 kg); max fuel, 9,281 lb (4 210 kg); max payload, 11,376 lb (5 160 kg); max take-off, 40,785 lb (18 500 kg); max zero fuel, 35,494 lb (16 100 kg); max landing, 39,683 lb (18 000 kg).

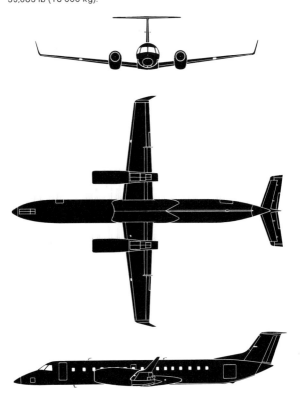

EMBRAER/FMA CBA-123 VECTOR

Dimensions: Span, 58 ft 1 in (17,72 m); overall length, 59 ft 5 in (18,09 m); overall height, 19 ft 7 in (5,97 m); wing area, 292.8 sq ft (27,2 m²).

Weights: Operating weight empty, 13,327 lb (6 045 kg); max payload, 4,751 lb (2 155 kg); max fuel, 4,547 lb (2 062 kg); max take-off, 19,929 lb (9 040 kg); max landing, 19,290 lb (8 750 kg); max zero fuel, 18,078 lb (8 200 kg).

EMBRAER/FMA CBA-123 VECTOR

Country of Origin: Brazil.
Type: Regional airliner.
Power Plant: Two Garrett TPF351-20 turbofans each rated at 1,300 shp (969 kW) for take-off.
Performance: Max cruising speed, 351 kts (650 km/h) at 24,000 ft (7 315 m); range with max payload, 780 naut mls (1 445 km); range with max fuel, 1,653 naut mls (3 062 km).
Accommodation: Flight crew of two. Standard layout for 19 passengers, three-abreast at 31-in (79-cm) seat pitch.
Status: Designed (as EMB-123, by Embraer) 1985/86. Launched on 21 May 1987 as joint Brazilian/Argentinian programme. Prototype first flown (in Brazil) on 18 July 1990 with second and third (in Brazil and Argentina respectively) by early 1991. Certification target October 1991 for initial customer delivery in December.
Sales: Orders/options for 150 from 18 customers in 13 countries, including 20 for Argentine Air Force.
Notes: The unconventionally-configured Vector was conceived by Embraer as a successor for the Bandeirante, production of which ended in 1990. Argentina, through FMA, has a 20 per cent share of the programme. Options include a number for corporate use, with eight–twelve passengers. Production go-ahead in 1991 awaited confirmation of 20 firm orders.

FAIRCHILD F-27 and FH-227

Country of Origin: USA.

Type: Short-range turboprop transport.

Power Plant (FH-227): Two 2,230 eshp (1 664 kW) Rolls-Royce Dart 532-7 or (FH-227D, E) 2,300 eshp (1 716 kW) Dart 532-7L turboprop engines.

Performance (FH-227E): Max cruising speed, 255 kts (473 km/h) at 15,000 ft (4 570 m); best economy cruise, 236 kts (435 km/h) at 25,000 ft (7 620 m); range with max payload, 570 naut mls (1 055 km); range with max fuel, 1,440 naut mls (2 660 km).

Accommodation: Flight crew of two (optionally, three) and up to 52 passengers four-abreast with central aisle at 31-in (79-cm) pitch, or a maximum of 56.

Status: Prototype Fairchild-built F27s flown 12 April and 23 May 1958; FAA certification 16 July 1958, entered service (West Coast Airlines) 27 September 1958. First FH-227 flown 27 January 1966; entered service (Mohawk) mid-1966. Production completed December 1968.

Sales: Fairchild built 128 F27s, plus a complete rebuild of first prototype after accidental damage, and 78 of the lengthened-fuselage FH-227s.

Notes: Fairchild acquired a licence to build the Fokker F27 (see separate entry) on 26 April 1956 and put the aircraft into production at the same time as the parent company, actually achieving first deliveries and airline service before Fokker's own Friendships. Variants up to F-27M were built or projected, all with the same basic dimensions and varying Dart models. Fairchild also was first to develop a stretched variant, as the FH-227, nearly two years before Fokker flew the first Mk 500, with slightly less 'stretch'.

FAIRCHILD F-27 and FH-227

Dimensions (FH-227): Span, 95 ft 2 in (29,00 m); length, 83 ft 8 in (25,50 m); height, 27 ft 7 in (8,41 m); wing area, 754 sq ft (70,0 m²).
Weights (FH-227): Operating weight empty, 22,923 lb (10 398 kg); max payload, 11,200 lb (5 080 kg); max fuel, 8,920 lb (4 046 kg); max zero fuel, 41,000 lb (18 600 kg); max take-off, 45,500 lb (20 639 kg); max landing, 45,000 lb (20 412 kg).

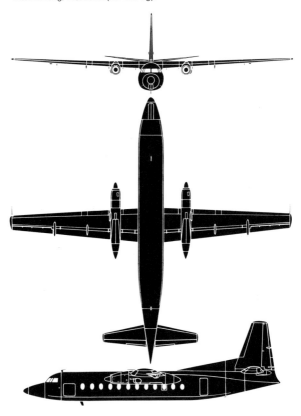

FAIRCHILD METRO III

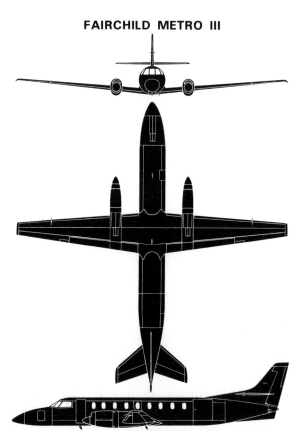

Dimensions: Span, 57 ft 0 in (17,37 m); length, 59 ft 4¼ in (18,09 m); height, 16 ft 8 in (5,08 m); wing area, 309 sq ft (28,71 m²).
Weights: Operating weight empty (III) 8,737 lb (3 963 kg), (IIIA), 8,823 lb (4 022 kg); max payload (III), 4,880 lb (2 214 kg); max zero fuel (III & IIIA), 12,500 lb (5 670 kg); max take-off (III & IIIA), 14,500 lb (6 577 kg); optional max take-off weight, 16,000 lb (7 257 kg); max landing (III & IIIA), 14,000 lb (6 350 kg); (optional) 15,500 lb (7 031 kg).

FAIRCHILD METRO III

Country of Origin: USA.

Type: Commuter airliner.

Power Plant: Two (Metro III) 1,000 shp (746 kW) Garrett TPE331-11U-612G turboprops, or (Metro IIIA) 1,100 shp (820 kW) Pratt & Whitney PT6A-45R turboprops.

Performance (Metro III): Max cruise, 278 kts (515 km/h) at 12,500 ft (3 810 m); long-range cruise, 256 kts (475 km/h) at 25,000 ft (7 620 m); max payload range (19 passengers), 575 naut mls (1 065 km) at cost econ cruise and 1,150 naut mls (2 131 km) at optional high gross weight.

Accommodation: Flight crew of two and 19 passengers at 30-in (76-cm) pitch two-abreast with central aisle.

Status: Metro prototype first flown 26 August 1969; certification 11 June 1970. Customer deliveries began 1973 (Air Wisconsin). Metro II introduced 1974; Metro IIA certificated to SFAR-41 23 June 1980. Metro III entered service 1981. Metro IIIA first flown 31 December 1981.

Sales: Approximately 400 Metros of all versions delivered by the beginning of 1991.

Notes: Metro III differs from earlier Metros in having a longer-span wing and more efficient engines, and Metro IIIA marks first use of Pratt & Whitney engines in this family of commuter aircraft. Both are certificated to SFAR-41B at weights shown. The name Expediter applies to an all-cargo version of the Metro III, with increased payload. Earlier Metro I and Metro II were limited to 12,500 lb (5 670 kg) gross weight by FAR Part 23 regulations. The name Merlin is used for variants of the basic Metro design furnished for corporate/business use. An improved corporate variant known as the Fairchild 400 was built only as a prototype as was the Metro 25 airliner; enlarged Metro V was abandoned. In 1991, Fairchild was working on the Metro 23C with TPE 331-11 or 1,100 shp (821 kW) TPE 331-12 turboprops and 16,500-lb (7 500-kg) gross weight.

FOKKER F27 FRIENDSHIP

Country of Origin: Netherlands.

Type: Short-range turboprop transport.

Power Plant: Two 2,280 ehp (1 700 kW) Rolls-Royce Dart 552 turboprops.

Performance: Max cruise at 38,000-lb (17 237-kg) weight, 259 kts (480 km/h) at 20,000 ft (6 100 m); long-range cruise, 232 kts (430 km/h) at 20,000 ft (6 100 m); range with max payload 1,285 naut mls (2 070 km); range with max fuel, 1,374 naut mls (2 211 km).

Accommodation: Flight crew of two (optionally, three) and up to 44 passengers four-abreast with central aisle at 30-in (76-cm) pitch.

Status: Two F27 prototypes first flown 24 November 1955 and 29 January 1957 respectively; US certification, 29 October 1957. First production F27 flown 23 March 1958; entered service (Mk 100 with Aer Lingus) 15 December 1958. Mk 200 first flown 20 September 1959; Mk 500 first flown 15 November 1967; Mk 600 first flown 28 November 1968.

Sales: Total of 581 F27s built by Fokker (and 205 by Fairchild as described separately), including about 200 military/government agency and corporate. Totals include 85 Mk 100, 138 Mk 200, 13 Mk 300, 218 Mk 400/600, 112 Mk 500 and 15 Maritime. Production ended in 1986 with two F27s for the Royal Thai Navy.

Notes: Fokker F27 is the best-selling turboprop airliner to date (excluding some Soviet types built in larger numbers). Major production versions are Mk 200, Mk 400 (primarily military) and Mk 500 (longer fuselage). The original Mk 100 had RDa6 engines, as did the Mk 300 Combiplane with side-loading freight door. The Fokker 50 is described separately on the next pages. *Photo:* Mk 500.

FOKKER F27 FRIENDSHIP

Dimensions (Mk 200): Span, 95 ft 2 in (29,00 m); length, 77 ft 3½ in (23,56 m); height, 27 ft 10¾ in (8,50 m); wing area, 754 sq ft (70,0 m²). **Weights** (Mk 200): Operating weight empty, 24,600 lb (11 159 kg); max payload, 10,340 lb (4 690 kg); max internal fuel, 13,180 lb (5 980 kg); max zero fuel, 39,500 lb (17,917 kg); max take-off, 45,000 lb (20 412 kg); max landing, 41,000 lb (18 598 kg).

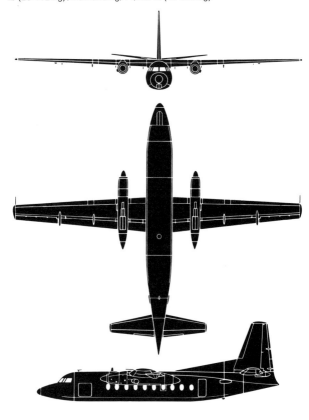

FOKKER 50

Dimensions: Span, 95 ft 1¾ in (29,00 m); overall length, 82 ft 10 in (25,25 m); overall height, 27 ft 3½ in (8,32 m); wing area, 753.5 sq ft (70,0 m²).
Weights: Operating weight empty, 27,712 lb (12 570 kg); max payload, 13,294 lb (6 030 kg); max fuel, 9,090 lb (4 123 kg); max take-off, 41,865 lb (18 990 kg); max landing, 41,865 lb (18 990 kg); max zero fuel, 41,000 lb (18 600 kg).

FOKKER 50

Country of Origin: Netherlands.

Type: Short-range turboprop transport.

Power Plant: Two Pratt & Whitney Canada PW125B turboprops each rated at 2,500 shp (1 864 kW) for take-off.

Performance: Max cruising speed, 287 kts (532 km/h) at 20,000 ft (6 100 m); economical cruise, 245 kts (454 km/h) at 25,000 ft (7 620 m); range with max payload, 674 naut mls (1 249 km); range at optional high gross weight, 1,635 naut mls (3 030 km).

Accommodation: Flight crew of two. Standard layout for 50 passengers, four-abreast. Max seating for 58, four-abreast at 30-in (76-cm) seat pitch.

Status: Two prototypes (converted from Fokker F27 airframes) flown on 28 December 1985 and 30 April 1986. First production aircraft flown 13 February 1987. Dutch certification (to JAR25) on 15 May 1987; FAA approval (to FAR25) 16 February 1989.

Sales: Total 126 (plus 14 options) to 17 operators/companies.

Notes: After studying a number of possible derivative versions of the F27 Friendship, Fokker announced in November 1983 its intention to proceed with development and production of this re-engined variant, named the Fokker 50 in line with its passenger capacity. The major innovation was to use Pratt & Whitney PW124 engines in place of Rolls-Royce Darts, but the Fokker 50 also has a number of other changes, with only some 20 per cent of components common with those of the F27. A lengthened Fokker 50-400 is under development, with 66 seats and PW127 engines. For introduction in 1994 or later, depending on market needs, the 50-400 has an overall length of 90 ft 8½ in (27,64 m).

FOKKER F28 FELLOWSHIP

Country of Origin: Netherlands.

Type: Regional jet airliner.

Power Plant: Two 9,900 lb st (44 kN) Rolls-Royce RB.183-2 Mk 555-15P turbofans.

Performance (Mk 4000 at 63,934 lb/29 000 kg gross weight): Max cruising speed, 436 kts (808 km/h) at 33,000 ft (10 058 m); long-range cruise, 354 kts (656 km/h) at 30,000 ft (9 150 m); range with max payload (85 passengers), long-range cruise, 1,125 naut mls (2 085 km).

Accommodation: Flight crew of two; max one-class seating for 85 passengers, five-abreast, at 29-in (74-cm) pitch.

Status: Prototypes first flown on 9 May and 3 August 1967 respectively; pre-production standard F28 flown 20 October 1967. Certification and first delivery (to LTU) 24 February 1969. Mk 6000 prototype flown 27 September 1973, not produced. First Mk 4000 long-fuselage variant flown 20 October 1976.

Sales: Total of 241 F28s sold (including military) to more than 50 operators by the end of 1986, when production ended.

Notes: F28 was developed and put into production as Fokker's first jet transport, to complement the highly successful F27 turboprop twin. The Mk 4000, for which data are given here, was of particular interest to regional airlines, and sold to such operators in the USA, the Far East, Africa and Europe. The Mk 2000 has the same fuselage length, Mk 1000 and Mk 3000 have a length of 43 ft 0 in (13,10 m) and up to 65 passengers. The Mks 5000 and 6000 were similar to the Mks 3000 and 4000 respectively, with leading-edge slats. The re-engined and stretched Fokker 100 is described separately on the next pages. *Photo:* F28 Mk 2000.

FOKKER F28 FELLOWSHIP

Dimensions: Span, 82 ft 3 in (25,07 m); length, 97 ft 1¾ in (29,61 m); height, 27 ft 9½ in (8,47 m); wing area, 850 sq ft (79,00 m²).
Weights: Operating weight empty, 38,683 lb (17 546 kg); max payload, 23,317 lb (10 576 kg); standard fuel, 17,240 lb (7 820 kg); max fuel, 23,080 lb (10 469 kg); max zero fuel, 62,000 lb (28 122 kg); max take-off, 73,000 lb (33 110 kg); max landing; 69,500 lb (31 524 kg).

FOKKER 100

Dimensions: Span, 92 ft 1½ in (28,08 m); overall length, 116 ft 6¾ in (35,53 m); overall height, 27 ft 10½ in (8,50 m); gross wing area, 1,006.4 sq ft (93,5 m²).

Weights: Operating weight empty, 53,700 lb (24 360 kg); max payload, 27,305 lb (12 385 kg); max take-off (Tay 620), 95,000 lb (43 090 kg); max take-off (Tay 650) 98,000 lb (44 450 kg); max landing, 88,000 lb (39 915 kg); max zero fuel, 81,000 lb (36 740 kg).

FOKKER 100

Country of Origin: Netherlands.
Type: Regional jet airliner.
Power Plant: Two 13,850 lb st (61,6 kN) Rolls-Royce Tay 620-15 or 15,100 lb st (67,2 kN) Tay 650-15 turbofans.
Performance: Max cruise, 465 kts (861 km/h) at 24,200 ft (7 375 m); economical cruise, 404 kts (748 km/h) at 35,000 ft (10 670 m); max operating altitude, 35,000 ft (10 670 m); range with max payload (107 passengers), 1,340 naut mls (2 483 km); range with max payload (high gross weight option); 1,600 naut mls (2 965 km).
Accommodation: Flight crew of two. Standard accommodation for 107 passengers five-abreast at 32-in (81-cm) pitch.
Status: Two prototypes flown on 30 November 1986 and 25 February 1987 respectively. First production aircraft flown 25 September 1987, certification 20 November, first customer delivery (Swissair) 29 February 1988, first revenue service 25 April 1988. First flight with Tay 650s, 8 June 1988.
Sales: Total 246 on firm order plus 128 options for 12 customers.
Notes: Fokker 100 is stretched derivative of F28, launched in late 1983. A high gross weight version, at 101,000 lb (45 815 kg) with Tay 650s, was introduced in 1990. Further development with uprated 18,000 lb st (80 kN) Tay 670s will allow gross weight increase to 104,000 lb (47 175 kg) and above. A lengthened version is also being studied by Fokker, based on the Tay 670, with a length of 137 ft (41,76 m) and span of 102 ft (31,09 m); known as the Fokker 130, it would have a gross weight of about 130,000 lb (59 000 kg) and eventually could be further developed to use BMW-RR BR720 engines.

GRUMMAN GULFSTREAM I

Country of Origin: USA.
Type: Short-to-medium range small-capacity commuterliner.
Power Plant: Two 1,990 shp (1 484 kW) Rolls-Royce Dart 529-8X or -8E turboprops.
Performance: Max cruising speed, 302 kts (560 km/h) at 25,000 ft (7 625 m); best economy cruising speed, 250 kts (463 km/h) at 25,000 ft (7 625 m); range with max fuel, 2,540 naut mls (4 088 km) with 2,740-lb (1 243-kg) payload.
Accommodation: Flight crew of two and up to 24 passengers two-abreast with single aisle.
Status: Gulfstream I first flown, as long-range corporate transport, on 14 August 1958. G-1C conversion by Gulfstream American first flown on 25 October 1979.
Sales: Total of 200 Gulfstream I built. About 25 in airline service in 1990. Five G-1C conversions made.
Notes: The Gulfstream I was the first corporate transport produced by Grumman (followed in due course by the Gulfstream II twin jet). Total production was for the business market but the type was later adopted in small numbers as a regional airliner with 20–24 seats. Users in 1990 included Aberdeen Airways and Birmingham European Airways in the UK, Air Provence in France (with 10), Indonesia Air Transport (with four) and operators in the US, Canada and Colombia. After Gulfstream American had acquired rights in the Grumman commercial aircraft, the G-1C was developed, with the fuselage lengthened by 11 ft 7 in (3,53 m), and up to 37 seats three-abreast.

GRUMMAN GULFSTREAM I

Dimensions: Span, 78 ft 6 in (23,92 m); length, 63 ft 9 in (19,43 m); height, 22 ft 9 in (6,94 m); wing area, 610.3 sq ft (56,7 m²).
Weights: Operating weight empty, 21,900 lb (9 933 kg); max payload, 4,270 lb (1 937 kg); max take-off, 35,100 lb (15 920 kg); max landing, 33,600 lb (15 240 kg); max zero fuel, 26,170 lb (11 870 kg).

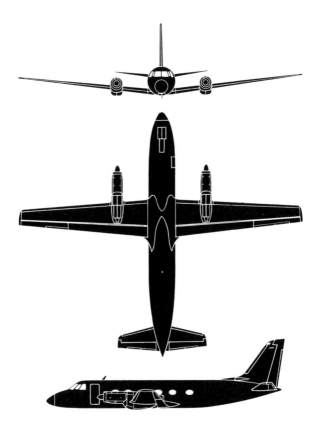

ILYUSHIN IL-18

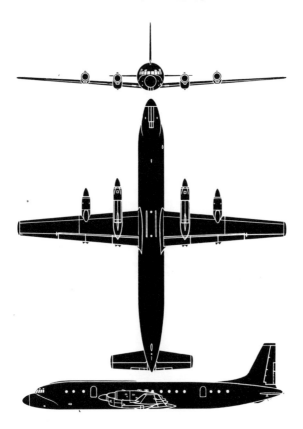

Dimensions: Span, 122 ft 8½ in (37,40 m); length, 117 ft 9 in (35,9 m); height, 33 ft 4 in (10,17 m); wing area, 1,507 sq ft (140 m²).
Weights: Empty equipped, 77,160 lb (35 000 kg); max payload, 29,750 lb (13 500 kg); max take-off, 141,100 lb (64 000 kg).

ILYUSHIN IL-18

Country of Origin: Soviet Union.

Type: Medium-range turboprop airliner.

Power Plant: Four 4,250 ehp (3 169 kW) Ivchenko AI-20M turbo-props.

Performance: Max cruising speed, 364 kts (675 km/h); economical cruising speed, 337 kts (625 km/h); range with max payload, 1,997 naut mls (3 700 km); range with max fuel, 3,508 naut mls (6 500 km).

Accommodation: Normal flight crew of five (two pilots, flight engineer, navigator and radio operator). Standard accommodation for 110 passengers in two cabins six-abreast and a rear compartment five-abreast. Max accommodation, 122.

Status: Prototype Il-18 first flown 4 July 1957; service use began (with Aeroflot) 20 April 1959. Production completed during 1968.

Sales: More than 600 Il-18s built, including approximately 100 exported to Communist Bloc countries in Europe, several African airlines, Cuba and China, and elsewhere.

Notes: A contemporary of the Antonov An-10, the Il-18 soon proved superior in the passenger-carrying rôle and in the two decades of the 'sixties and the 'seventies it played a major rôle in the expansion and modernization of Aeroflot services within the Soviet Union and on international services in Europe and the Middle East. The 84-passenger Il-18V was the initial standard version, with 4,000 ehp (2 983 kW) AI-20K engines; the Il-18E had more power and a revised interior, and the Il-18D (data above) had increased fuel and a higher gross weight.

ILYUSHIN IL-62

Country of Origin: Soviet Union.

Type: Long-range jet transport.

Power Plant: Four (Il-62) 23,150 lb st (103 kN) Kuznetsov NK-8-4 or (Il-62M) 24,250 lb st (107,9 kN) Soloviev D-30KU turbofans.

Performance (Il-62M): Typical cruising speed, 442–486 kts (820–900 km/h) at 35,000 ft (10 670 m); range with max payload, 4,210 naut mls (7 800 km); range with payload of 22,045 lb (10 000 kg), 5,400 naut mls (10 000 km).

Accommodation: Flight crew of five (two pilots, flight engineer, navigator and radio operator); maximum accommodation in two cabins for 186 passengers (174 in Il-62M, 195 in Il-62MK), six-abreast at a pitch of 34 in (86 cm) with central aisle.

Status: Prototype first flown January 1963 (with Lyulka AL-7 engines); service introduction (with Aeroflot) 15 September 1967. Il-62M first flown 1971 and entered service 1974; Il-62MK introduced 1978.

Sales: Production of 250 (complete) included about 75 exported to East European and other airlines in the Soviet sphere of influence.

Notes: The Il-62 was the first Soviet jetliner designed for long-range intercontinental operations. The original production version was powered by Kuznetsov NK-8-4 turbofans but the improved Il-62M, appearing in 1971, has Soloviev D-30s of greater thrust and lower specific fuel consumption, combined with a fin fuel tank for longer range. The Il-62MK has a higher gross weight (368,170 lb/167 000 kg), increasing payload to 195 passengers.

ILYUSHIN IL-62

Dimensions: Span, 141 ft 9 in (43,20 m); length, 174 ft 3½ in (53,12 m); height, 40 ft 6¼ in (12,35 m); wing area, 3,009 sq ft (279,55 m).
Weights: Operating weight empty, approximately 157,630 lb (71 500 kg); max payload, 50,700 lb (23 000 kg); max zero fuel, 208,550 lb (94 600 kg); max take-off, 363,760 lb (165 000 kg); max landing, 231,500 kg (105 000 kg).

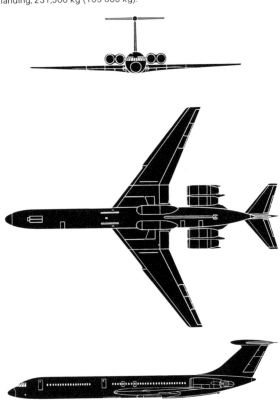

ILYUSHIN IL-86

Dimensions: Span, 157 ft 8¼ in (48,06 m); length, 195 ft 4 in (59,54 m); height, 51 ft 10½ in (15,81 m); wing area, 3,444 sq ft (320 m²).
Weights: Max payload, 92,600 lb (42 000 kg); max fuel load, 189,600 lb (86 000 kg); max take-off, 458,560 lb (208 000 kg); max landing, 385,800 lb (175 000 kg).

ILYUSHIN IL-86

Country of Origin: Soviet Union.

Type: Long-range jetliner.

Power Plant: Four 28,660 lb st (127,5 kN) Kuznetsov NK-86 turbofans.

Performance: Max cruising speed, 512 kts (950 km/h) at 35,000 ft (10 670m); economical cruise, 486 kts (900 km/h) at 35,000 ft (10 670m); design range with payload of 88,185 lb (40 000 kg), 1,945 naut mls (3 600 km); design range with max fuel, 2,480 naut mls (4 600 km).

Accommodation: Normal flight crew of three (two pilots and flight engineer) plus provision for navigator. Maximum of 350 passengers, nine-abreast with two aisles; typical mixed class layout, 28 six-abreast in forward cabin and 206 eight-abreast in main and rear cabins.

Status: First of two prototypes flown at Moscow on 22 December 1976. First production-configured aircraft flown 24 October 1977. Proving flights began September 1978 and first scheduled service flown by Aeroflot 26 December 1980, and first international service (Moscow–East Berlin) 3 July 1981.

Sales: About 70 in service with Aeroflot with production expected to continue to about 100 aircraft. No exports.

Notes: The Il-86 is the Soviet Union's first 'airbus' type with a twin-aisle layout in the wide-body cabin; at first projected with a rear-engined layout, it was eventually built in the form illustrated after analysis showing the structural weight penalties and low-speed handling difficulties of the former. Major Il-86 airframe components are produced in Poland, and final assembly takes place at Voronezh in the USSR. A version with Soloviev PS-90A turbofans was under development in 1990 and was expected to overcome the range deficiencies of the NK-86 powered version described here. Ilyushin was also studying a programme to re-engine Il-86s with General Electric/SNECMA CFM56 turbofans.

ILYUSHIN IL-96-300

Country of Origin: Soviet Union.

Type: Long-range large-capacity jet transport.

Power Plant: Four Soloviev PS-90A (D-90) turbofans each rated at 35,275 lb st (156,9 kN) for take-off.

Performance (Il-96-300): Max cruise, 486 kts (900 km/h) at 35,000 ft (10 670 m); economical cruise, 459 kts (850 km/h) at 35,000 ft (10 670 m); max operating altitude, 39,400 ft (12 000 m); range with max passenger payload, 4,860 naut mls (9 000 km); range with max fuel (33,000 lb/15 000 kg payload), 5,950 naut mls (11 000 km).

Accommodation: Flight crew of three (two pilots and flight engineer). Typical three-class layout for 22F + 40B + 173E, respectively six, eight and nine-abreast. Max passengers 300, nine-abreast at 34.5-in (87-cm) pitch.

Status: First of three prototype/development aircraft flown on 28 September 1988 at Khodinka. Second aircraft flown on 28 November 1989. Introduction into service with Aeroflot expected during 1991.

Sales: Production of about 65 planned in 1990–95 five-year plan against known Aeroflot requirement for at least 100.

Notes: Of similar overall configuration to the Il-86, the Il-96 has little else in common with the former type except the cabin cross-section. Lower structural weight, a shorter fuselage and more efficient engines bestow on the Il-96 an improved payload/range performance. A lengthened version was under development in 1990 as the Il-96M, with a 30 ft 8 in (9,35-m) stretch, 375 seats, a range of 6,400 naut mls (11 800 km) and Pratt & Whitney PW2037 turbofans specified as the preferred engines.

ILYUSHIN IL-96-300

Dimensions: Span, 189 ft 2 in (57,66 m); length, 181 ft 7¼ in (55,35 m); height, 57 ft 7¾ in (17,57 m); gross wing area, 4,215 sq ft (391,6 m²).

Weights: Operating weight empty, 258,000 lb (117 000 kg); max fuel, 269,000 lb (122 000 kg); max payload, 88,200 lb (40 000 kg); max take-off, 476,200 lb (216 000 kg); max landing, 385,800 lb (175 000 kg); max zero fuel, 346,120 lb (157 000 kg).

ILYUSHIN IL-114

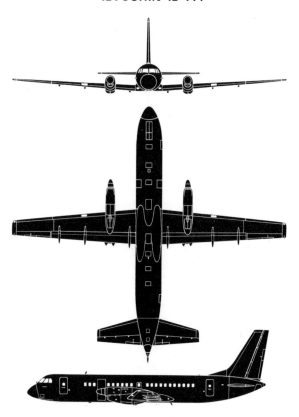

Dimensions: Span, 98 ft 5¼ in (30,0 m); overall length, 86 ft 4 in (26,31 m); overall height, 30 ft 7 in (9,32 m).

Weights: Operating weight empty, 30,200 lb (13 700 kg); max payload, 13,227 lb (6 000 kg); max fuel, 14,330 lb (6 500 kg); max take-off, 46,300 lb (21 000 kg).

ILYUSHIN IL-114

Country of Origin: Soviet Union.
Type: Regional turboprop airliner.
Power Plant: Two Leningrad Design Bureau TV7-117 turboprops each rated at 2,368 shp (1 766 kW) for take-off.
Performance: Typical cruising speed, 270 kts (500 km/h) at 19,700 ft (6 000 m); range with max payload, 450 naut mls (835 km); range with 3,300-lb (1 500-kg) payload, 2,590 naut mls (4 800 km).
Accommodation: Flight crew of two. Typical layout for 60 passengers, four-abreast. Max seating for 68, four-abreast at 29.5-in (75-cm) seat pitch.
Status: Design definition completed 1986. First flown 29 March 1990 at Zhukovsky, near Moscow. Final assembly line for production aircraft at Tashkent.
Sales: Approximately 500 required by Aeroflot in 1990/95 five-year plan.
Notes: The Il-114 was designed as a successor for the Antonov An-24, to serve on Aeroflot routes with ranges of up to about 540 naut mls (1 000 km), and became one of a trio of types that were under development in the late 'eighties to provide for modernization of the Aeroflot fleet in the 'nineties. The Il-114—which is strikingly similar to the British Aerospace ATP, an aircraft in the same class—makes much use of composite materials and advanced metal alloys, including titanium, in its structure, which is designed to have a fatigue life of 30,000 hrs and 30,000 landings. Avionics and flight systems are of a standard to allow the Il-114 to operate in weather minima down to ICAO Cat II standard. The Polish, Romanian and Bulgarian aircraft industries are participating in production of the Il-114. Preliminary plans have been made for a lengthened version to seat 70–75 passengers.

LET L-410

Country of Origin: Czechoslovakia.
Type: Light turboprop transport.
Power Plant: Two 750 ehp (559 kW) Motorlet (Walter) M 601E turboprops.
Performance: Max cruise, 197 kts (365 km/h); economical cruise, 162 kts (300 km/h); range with max payload, 210 naut mls (390 km); range with max fuel, 561 naut mls (1 040 km).
Accommodation: Flight crew of two and up to 19 passengers three-abreast with off-set aisle at 30-in (76-cm) pitch.
Status: Prototype L-410 flown on 16 April 1969. First L-410M flown 1973. Prototype L-410 UVP flown 1 November 1977, certificated and entered service 1980. L-410 UVP-E first flown 30 December 1984.
Sales: Primary customer is Aeroflot, which took delivery of its 500th L-410 in March 1985. More than 1,000 built by end 1990, of which 897 delivered to Aeroflot.
Notes: Development of the L-410 light transport began at the Kunovice works of the Let National Corporation (Let Národni Podnik) in 1966, as the first complete aircraft project undertaken by that factory. The first 31 aircraft were completed as L-410As with Pratt & Whitney PT6A-27 engines and saw some service with CSA and Slov-Air, as did the L-410M with M-601A engines (110 built). Variants of these two basic types included the L-410AF aerial survey version, the L-410AS with Soviet-specified avionics, the L-410MA with M-601B engines and the L-410MU with Soviet-specified changes. The L-410 UVP is the definitive production version, adopted by Aeroflot for use on regional services; this has a slightly longer fuselage, dihedral on the tailplane and numerous other improvements. The L-410 UVP-E has five-bladed propellers, tip tanks and internal changes to increase seating from 15 to 19. *Photo:* L-410 UVP-E.

LET L-410

Dimensions: Span, 63 ft 10¾ in (19,48 m); (UVP-E, over tip tanks), 65 ft 6½ in (19,98 m); length, 47 ft 4 in (14,42 m); height, 19 ft 1½ in (5,83 m); wing area, 378.67 sq ft (35,18 m²).

Weights (UVP-E): Operating weight empty, 9,171 lb (4 160 kg); max fuel, 2,866 lb (1 300 kg); max payload, 3,560 lb (1 615 kg); max take-off, 14,110 lb (6 400 kg); max landing, 13,668 lb (6 200 kg); max zero fuel, 12,732 lb (5 775 kg).

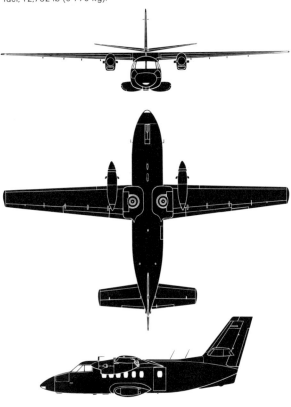

LET L-610

Dimensions: Span, 84 ft 0 in (25,60 m); overall length, 70 ft 3¼ in (21,42 m); overall height, 24 ft 11½ in (7,6 m); wing area, 602.8 sq ft (56,0 m²).

Weights: Operating weight empty, 19,841 lb (9 000 kg); max payload, 8,377 lb (3 800 kg); max fuel, 5,842 lb (2 650 kg); max take-off, 30,865 lb (14 000 kg); max landing, 29,762 lb (13 500 kg); max zero fuel, 28,219 lb (12 800 kg).

LET L-610

Country of Origin: Czechoslovakia.

Type: Short-haul regional airliner.

Power Plant: Two Motorlet M 602 turboprops each rated at 1,822 shp (1 358 kW) for take-off.

Performance: Max cruising speed, 264 kts (490 km/h) at 23,620 ft (7 200 m); economical cruise, 220 kts (408 km/h) at 23,620 ft (7 200 m); range with max payload, 469 naut mls (870 km); range with max fuel, 1,298 naut mls (2 406 km).

Accommodation: Flight crew of two. Standard layout for 40 passengers, four-abreast at 29.5-in (75-cm) seat pitch.

Status: Design definition of L-610 was completed in the mid 'eighties. Prototype first flown on 28 December 1988, with two more assigned to flight test programme, for certification by end-1990 and first deliveries (to Aeroflot) early 1991. Production planned at 15 in 1991, 20 in 1992 and then 40 per year. First flight with CT7 engines scheduled for September 1991.

Sales: Aeroflot has a stated requirement for 600.

Notes: L-610 resembles an enlarged L-410, the successful light twin of which some 900 have been built to date, particularly for use in the Soviet Union—where the L-610 will also be operated in substantial numbers. For the Western market, a version with General Electric CT7-9B turboprops is under development, and an improved version of the M 602 engine was fitted for testing in one of the prototypes in mid-1990. The first two production L-610s were delivered to Aeroflot in the Soviet Union early in 1991 for the completion of certification flying.

LOCKHEED L-1011-100, -200 TRISTAR

Country of Origin: USA.

Type: Medium-long-range large-capacity airliner.

Power Plant: Three (-1, -100) 42,000 lb st (186,8 kN) Rolls-Royce RB.211-22B or (-200) 50,000 lb st (222,4 kN) RB.211-524 turbofans.

Performance (L-1011-200): Max cruising speed at mid-cruise weight, 526 kts (973 km/h) at 30,000 ft (9 145 m); economical cruising speed, 463 kts (890 km/h) at 35,000 ft (10 670 m); range with max passenger payload, 5,812 naut mls (6 690 km); range with max fuel, 4,918 naut mls (9 111 km).

Accommodation: Flight crew of three and up to 400 passengers 10-abreast with two aisles, at 30-in (76-cm) seat pitch; typical mixed-class, 256, basically nine-abreast.

Status: First L-1011 flown 17 November 1970 and fifth, completing the development batch, on 2 December 1971. Provisional certification 22 December 1971; full certification 14 April 1972 and first service (Eastern) 30 April. First flight with RB.211-524 engines, 12 August 1976, certification of -200 on 26 April 1977 and entered service with Saudia. Production completed 1984.

Sales: Total of 249 built for 16 airlines (including L-1011-500, see next entry), plus one company-owned prototype. Eighteen airlines operating -1, -100, and -200 models in 1987.

Notes: Lockheed launched the Tristar in March 1968 as the second of the wide-body transports. The -100 differs from the original -1 in having higher weights and more fuel, while the -200 is like the -100 but with uprated engines. The -250 is a -1 conversion with RB.211-524B4 engines. *Photo:* L-1011-100.

LOCKHEED L-1011 TRISTAR

Dimensions: Span, 155 ft 4 in (47,34 m); length, 177 ft 8½ in (54,17 m); height, 55 ft 4 in (16,87 m); wing area, 3,456 sq ft (320,0 m²).
Weights (-200): Operating weight empty, 248,000 lb (112 670 kg); max payload, 89,600 lb (40 642 kg); max fuel weight, 176,930 lb (80 254 kg); max zero fuel, 338,000 lb (153 315 kg); max take-off, 466,000 lb (211 375 kg); max landing, 368,000 lb (166 920 kg).

LOCKHEED L-1011-500 TRISTAR

Dimensions: Span, 164 ft 4 in (50,09 m); length, 164 ft 2½ in (50,05 m); height, 55 ft 4 in (16,87 m); wing area, 3,540 sq ft (329,0 m²).
Weights: Operating weight empty, 245,400 lb (111 311 kg); max payload, 92,608 lb (42 006 kg); max fuel weight, 211,249 lb (95 821 kg); max zero fuel, 338,000 lb (153 315 kg); max take-off, 510,000 lb (231 330 kg); max landing, 368,000 lb (166 920 kg).

LOCKHEED L-1011-500 TRISTAR

Country of Origin: USA.

Type: Long-range large-capacity airliner.

Power Plant: Three 50,000 lb st (222,4 kN) Rolls-Royce RB.211-524B or B4 turbofans.

Performance: Max cruising speed at mid-cruise weight, 518 kts (959 km/h) at 33,000 ft (10 000 m); economical cruising speed, 483 kts (894 km/h) at 35,000 ft (10 670 m); range with max passenger payload, 5,345 naut mls (9 905 km); range with max fuel, 6,100 naut mls (11 260 km).

Accommodation: Flight crew of three and up to 330 passengers 10-abreast with two aisles at 30/33-in (76/83-cm) pitch; typical mixed class, 24F (six-abreast) and 222E (nine-abreast).

Status: First L-1011-500 flown 16 October 1978; extended wingtips first flown (on original L-1011-1 prototype) in 1978 and on production -500 (with active ailerons) in November 1979. Entered service (British Airways, without active controls) 7 May 1979 and (Pan American, with active controls) early 1980. Certificated with fully-digital flight control system for Cat IIIA operations, 17 June 1981. Production completed 1984.

Sales: Approximately 50 sold to 10 airlines within overall TriStar production total of 250 (see previous entry).

Notes: The TriStar 500 was launched in August 1976 as a derivative of the -200 (see previous entry), to provide a transport of longer range and reduced capacity. It features active controls to reduce wing bending moments, an improved wing-to-fuselage fairing and an advanced flight management system. Wing span is increased and fuselage length reduced. *Photo:* L-1011-500.

McDONNELL DOUGLAS DC-8

Country of Origin: USA.

Type: Long-range medium-capacity turbofan transport.

Power Plant (Srs 70): Four 22,000 lb st (97,9 kN) CFM International CFM56-2-C5 turbofans.

Performance (Srs 73): Max cruising speed, 479 kts (887 km/h) at 39,000 ft (11 890 m); best economy cruising speed, 459 kts (850 km/h) at 39,000 ft (11 890 m); range with max payload, 4,830 naut mls (8 950 km).

Accommodation (Srs 73): Flight crew of three and up to 269 passengers six-abreast with central aisle at 30-in (76-cm) pitch.

Status First flights: Srs 10, 30 May 1958; Srs 20, 29 November 1958; Srs 30, 21 February 1959; Srs 40, 23 July 1959; Srs 50, 20 December 1960; Srs 55 Jet Trader, 20 October 1962; Srs 61, 14 March 1966; Srs 62, 29 August 1966; Srs 63, 10 April 1967; Srs 71, 15 August 1981; Srs 72, 5 December 1981; Srs 73, 4 March 1982. Entry into service: Srs 10 (Delta, United) 18 September 1959; Srs 30 (Pan American) April 1960; Srs 40 (TCA) April 1960; Srs 61, 25 February 1967; Srs 62, 22 May 1967; Srs 63, 27 July 1967; Srs 71, 24 April 1982. Production completed, May 1972.

Sales: One prototype (unsold) and 555 DC-8s built, comprising 28 Srs 10, 24 Srs 20, 57 Srs 30, 32 Srs 40, 87 Srs 50, 54 Srs 55, 88 Srs 61, 68 Srs 62 and 107 Srs 63. 110 Sixty-series converted to Srs 70 versions. About 250 DC-8s remain in service in 1991, principally Srs 50, 60 and 70.

Notes: Srs 10 to 50 were dimensionally similar to each other, with varying power plants, fuel capacity and weights; Srs 55 Jet Trader had cargo door. Srs 61 and 63 had 36 ft 8 in (11,18-m) fuselage stretch and Srs 62 had 6 ft 8 in (2,03-m) stretch. Srs 71, 72, 73 are conversions of 60-series with CFM56 engines. *Photo:* DC-8 Srs 61.

McDONNELL DOUGLAS DC-8

Dimensions (Srs 73): Span, 148 ft 5 in (45,20 m); length, 187 ft 5 in (57,1 m); height, 43 ft 0 in (13,1 m); wing area, 2,927 sq ft (271,9 m²).
Weights (Srs 73): Operating weight empty, 166,500 lb (75 500 kg), max payload, 64,500 lb (29 257 kg); max fuel, 162,642 lb (73 773 kg); max take-off, 355,000 lb (161 025 kg); max landing, 258,000 lb (117 000 kg).

McDONNELL DOUGLAS DC-9 SRS 10–30

Dimensions (Srs 30): Span, 93 ft 5 in (28,47 m); overall length, 119 ft 3½ in (36,37 m); overall height, 27 ft 6 in (8,38 m); wing area, 1,000.7 sq ft (92,97 m²).

Weights (Srs 30): Operating weight empty, 57,190 lb (25 940 kg); max payload, 31,000 lb (14 060 kg); max take-off 121,000 lb (54 885 kg); max landing, 110,000 lb (49 895 kg); max zero fuel, 98,500 lb (44 678 kg).

McDONNELL DOUGLAS DC-9 SRS 10–30

Country of Origin: USA.

Type: Short-to-medium-range jet transport.

Power Plant (Srs 30): Two 14,500 lb st (64,5 kN) Pratt & Whitney JT8D-9 or 15,000 lb st (66,7 kN) JT8D-11 or 15,500 lb st (68,9 kN) JT8D-15 or 16,000 lb st (71,2 kN) JT8D-17 turbofans.

Performance (Srs 30): Max cruising speed, 490 kts (907 km/h) at 25,000 ft (7 620 m); economical cruise, 431 kts (798 km/h) at 35,000 ft (10 670 m); range with 80 passengers, 1,670 naut mls (3 095 km).

Accommodation (Srs 30): Flight crew of two. Max seating for 115, five-abreast at 32-in (81-cm) seat pitch.

Status: First (Srs 10) development aircraft flown 25 February 1965; first Srs 30 flown 1 August 1966; first Srs 20 flown 18 September 1968. DC-9RF development aircraft (JT8D-109 engines) flown 9 January 1975. Certification: (Srs 10), 23 November 1965; (Srs 20), 11 December 1968; (Srs 30), 19 December 1966. Entry into service: Srs 10 (Delta), 8 December 1965; Srs 20 (SAS), 23 January 1969; Srs 30 (Eastern), 1 February 1967.

Sales: Total of 976 DC-9s built, including 137 Srs 10, 10 Srs 20 and 662 Srs 30 (of which 43 for military users). See also next entry for Srs 40 and Srs 50.

Notes: The DC-9 was launched by Douglas Aircraft Co (then independent) on 8 April 1963, to complement the DC-8, and Delta Air Lines became the launch customer soon after. With 12,000 lb st (53,4 kN) JT8D-5 engines, the initial Srs 10 had an overall length of 104 ft 4¾ in (31,82 cm) and up to 90 seats, but the Srs 30 (data above) soon became the principal variant. The Srs 20 combined the Srs 10 fuselage with JT8D-9 or -11 engines and the longer span of the Srs 30 wing with full-span leading-edge slats, for 'hot and high' operations. Convertible (C) and all-freight (F) versions of the Srs 10 and Srs 30 were also delivered. *Photo:* DC-9-15.

McDONNELL DOUGLAS DC-9
SRS 40 and 50

Country of Origin: USA.

Type: Short-to-medium-range jet transport.

Power Plant (Srs 50): Two 15,000 lb st (66,7 kN) Pratt & Whitney JT8D-15 or 16,000 lb st (71,2 kN) JT8D-17 turbofans.

Performance (Srs 50): Max cruising speed, 501 kts (929 km/h) at 27,000 ft (8 230 m); long-range cruising speed, 440 kts (817 km/h) at 35,000 ft (10 670 m); range with 97-passenger payload, 1,796 naut mls (3 326 km).

Accommodation (Srs 50): Flight crew of two and up to 139 passengers five-abreast with offset aisle at 31-in (79-cm) pitch.

Status: Srs 40 first flown on 28 November 1967, certificated 27 February 1968, entered service (SAS) 12 March 1968. Srs 50 first flown 17 December 1974, entered service (Swissair) 24 August 1975.

Sales: Total of 976 DC-9s built, including 40 Srs 71 and 96 Srs 50. Series 80 redesignated MD-80 (see next entry).

Notes: To meet the specific needs of SAS, Douglas 'stretched' the DC-9 for the second time by adding 6 ft 4 in (1,87 m) to the overall length of the Srs 30. This produced the Srs 40, with up to 125 seats. Then in 1973 Swissair became the launch customer for yet another 'stretch', which again added 6 ft 4 in (1,87 m) to the previous longest version and produced the Srs 50. Further evolution, based upon engine improvements offered by Pratt & Whitney, led to a DC-9 Super 80; this was re-designated MD-80 before customer deliveries began and is described in the next entry. *Photo:* DC-9-51.

McDONNELL DOUGLAS DC-9 SRS 40 and 50

Dimensions (Srs 50): Span, 93 ft 5 in (28,47 m); length, 119 ft 3½ in (36,37 m); height, 27 ft 6 in (8,38 m); wing area, 1,000.7 sq ft (92,97 m²).

Weights (Srs 50): Operating weight empty, 57,190 lb (25 940 kg); max payload, 31,000 lb (14 060 kg); max take-off, 121,000 lb (54 885 kg); max landing, 110,000 lb (49 895 kg).

McDONNELL DOUGLAS MD-80

Dimensions: Span, 107 ft 10 in (32,87 m); length, 147 ft 10 in (45,06 m); height, 29 ft 8 in (9,03 m); wing area, 1,270 sq ft (118 m²).
Weights (MD-81): Operating weight empty, 78,420 lb (35 570 kg); max payload, 39,579 lb (17 952 kg); max fuel, 39,128 lb (17 748 kg); max zero fuel, 118,000 lb (53 524 kg); max take-off, 140,000 lb (63 500 kg); max landing, 128,000 lb (58 060 kg). (MD-83/88), max take-off, 160,000 lb (72 575 kg).

McDONNELL DOUGLAS MD-80

Country of Origin: USA.

Type: Short-to-medium-range jet transport.

Power Plant: Two (MD-81) 18,500 lb st (82,3 kN) Pratt & Whitney JT8D-209 turbofans with 750 lb st (3,3 kN) emergency reserve (ETR) or (MD-82) 20,000 lb st (89 kN) JT8D-217 with ETR of 850 lb st (3,8 kN) or (MD-83/88) 21,000 lb st (93,4 kN) JT8D-219 turbofans.

Performance: Max cruise, 478 kts (885 km/h) at 27,000 ft (8 230 m); long-range cruise, 439 kts (813 km/h) at 35,000 ft (10 670 m); range with 115-passenger payload (MD-81) 1,563 naut mls (2 896 km), (MD-82) 2,040 naut mls (3 778 km); (MD-83) 2,500 naut mls (4 635 km).

Accommodation: Flight crew of two and up to 172 passengers five-abreast, at 31-in (78-cm) seat pitch.

Status: Development MD-80s first flown on 18 October 1979, 6 December 1979 and 29 February 1980; MD-82 flown 8 January 1981; MD-83 flown 17 December 1984; first MD-88 flown 15 August 1987. MD-81 certification 30 July 1981, entry into service (Swissair) 5 October 1980. MD-82 certification 30 July 1981, entry into service (Republic) August 1982. MD-83 certificated November 1985 and entry into service with Finnair. MD-88 certificated 9 December 1987, entered service (Delta) 5 January 1988.

Sales: Total of about 1,400 orders and commitments for MD-80 variants by early 1991, including about 180 MD-81, 670 MD-82, 270 MD-83 and 170 MD-88.

Notes: The MD-80 was launched as the DC-9 Super 80 in October 1977, as a 'stretched' Srs 50. The MD-81, 82, 83 and 88 are dimensionally similar, with different engines, fuel options and weights. MD-87 is shorter (see next entry). *Photo:* MD-82.

McDONNELL DOUGLAS MD-87

Country of Origin: USA.
Type: Short-to-medium-range jet transport.
Power Plant: Two 20,000 lb st (88,9 kN) Pratt & Whitney JT8D-217C turbofans with 850-lb (3,8-kN) thrust reserve.
Performance: Max speed, 500 kts (925 km/h); long-range cruising speed, 438 kts (811 km/h) at 35,000 ft (10 670 m); range with 130-passenger payload, 2,370 naut mls (4 395 km); range with auxiliary fuel, 2,833 naut mls (5 246 km).
Accommodation: Flight crew of two and up to 130 passengers five-abreast with offset aisle at 32-in (81-cm) pitch.
Status: Launch decision announced 3 January 1985 following purchase decision by Finnair and Austrian taken in December 1984. First prototype flown 4 December 1986, certificated 21 October 1987, entered service with Finnair and Austrian.
Sales: Total of 130 ordered by early 1991, within overall total of about 1,400 orders and commitments for MD-80 variants.
Notes: The MD-87 was developed in the mid-eighties to combine the advanced features of the MD-80 series (see previous entry) with the shorter fuselage of the original DC-9 Srs 30, in order to provide an economic twin jet of smaller capacity than the earlier 155-seat MD-80s. The fuselage of the MD-87 is 17 ft 5 in (5,3 m) shorter than that of the basic MD-80 series, providing for a typical mixed-class layout with 117 seats. A small upward extension of the fin above the tailplane compensates for the shorter moment arm, but in all other respects the MD-87 is externally identical to its long-fuselage forerunners.

McDONNELL DOUGLAS MD-87

Dimensions: Span, 107 ft 9½ in (32.86 m); length, 130 ft 5 in (39.7 m); height, 30 ft 6 in (9.29 m); wing area, 1,209 sq ft (112.0 m²).
Weights: Operating weight empty, 73,274 lb (33 237 kg); max payload, 30,820 lb (13 980 kg); max fuel, 39,130 lb (17 750 kg); max take-off, 140,000 lb (63 503 kg); optional max take-off, 149,500 lb (67 813 kg); max landing, 128,000 lb (58 060 kg).

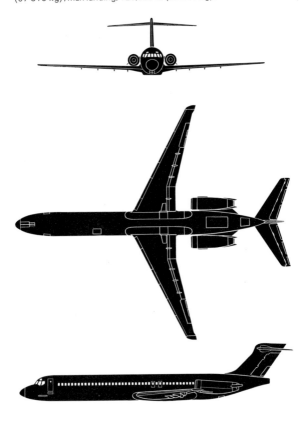

McDONNELL DOUGLAS MD-90

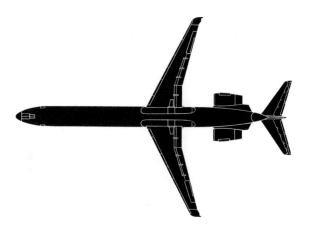

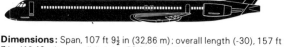

Dimensions: Span, 107 ft 9½ in (32,86 m); overall length (-30), 157 ft 7 in (46,40 m); overall height, 30 ft 11 in (9,40 m); gross wing area, 1,209 sq ft (112 m²).
Weights: Operating weight empty, 86,882 lb (39 409 kg); max take-off, 156,000 lb (70 748 kg); max landing, 122,000 lb (55 329 kg); max zero fuel, 114,000 lb (51 701 kg).

McDONNELL DOUGLAS MD-90

Country of Origin: USA.

Type: Medium-range jet transport.

Power Plant: Two (MD-90-10) 22,000 lb st (97,86 kN) IAE V2522-D5 or (MD-90-30) 25,000 lb st (111,2 kN) V2525-D5 or (MD-90-40) 28,000 lb st (124,6 kN) V2528-D5 turbofans.

Performance: Typical cruise, 438 kts (811 km/h) at 35,000 ft (10 670 m); range with full payload (153 passengers), (-30), 2,388 naut mls (4 415 km), (-10), 2,415 naut mls (4 475 km), (-40), 1,740 naut mls (3 226 km).

Accommodation (-30): Flight crew of two. Typical mixed class layout for 12 + 141 passengers. Maximum high density arrangement, 172 passengers (181 in -40EC).

Status: Programme launched 14 November 1989. First flight early 1993, to achieve certification in time for first airline deliveries (Delta and Alaska Airlines) in fourth quarter of 1994. MD-90-40EC certification, second-half 1995, and -30EC first quarter 1996.

Sales: Total of 139 firm sales by early 1991, plus 199 options, to more than four customers.

Notes: MD-90 designation was first used for a short-body version of the MD-80 (later launched as MD-87) and was then applied to a family of MD-80 derivatives and all-new proposals using aft-mounted propfans. Eventually, in late 1989, MD-90 family was launched as a continuation of the MD-80 series, using IAE V2500 engines. The Srs 10, 30 and 40 have differing fuselage lengths and engine thrusts. Also in the definition phase is an MD-90EC (Enhanced Configuration) with more wing area, more advanced cockpit, greater passenger capacity (up to 190) and other improvements, aimed primarily at European operations. Srs 20 designation would apply to V2500 retrofits on MD-80 variants. *Photo:* MD-90-30.

McDONNELL DOUGLAS DC-10

Country of Origin: USA.

Type: Medium-long-range large-capacity airliner.

Power Plant: Three (Srs 30) 49,000 lb st (218 kN) General Electric CF6-50A or 51,000 lb st (226,9 kN) CF6-50C or 52,500 lb st (233,5 kN) CF6-50C1 or C2 turbofans or 54,000 lb st (240,2 kN) CF6-50C2B or (Srs 40) 49,400 lb st (219,6 kN) Pratt & Whitney JT9D-20 or 53,000 lb st (235,8 kN) JT9D-59A turbofans.

Performance (Srs 30): Max cruise, 490 kts (908 km/h) at 30,000 ft (9 154 m); long-range cruise, 475 kts (880 km/h) at 31,000 ft (9 450 m); range with max payload, 4,000 naut mls (7 413 km); ferry range with max fuel (zero payload), 6,504 naut mls (12 055 km).

Accommodation: Flight crew of three and up to 380 passengers ten-abreast with two aisles at 32-in (81-cm) seat pitch.

Status: First three development DC-10s (Srs 10s) flown 29 August, 24 October and 23 December 1970; certificated 29 July 1971, entered service (American Airlines) 5 August 1971. Srs 15 first flown 8 January 1981, certificated 12 June 1981, entered service with Aeromexico. Srs 30 first flown 21 June 1972, certificated 21 November 1972, entered service with KLM and Swissair. Srs 30CF flown 28 February 1973, first deliveries (to TIA and ONO) April 1973. Srs 40 first flown 28 February 1972, certificated 20 October 1972, entered service with Northwest Orient.

Sales: Total of 386 commercial DC-10s, plus 60 KC-10A military tankers. Production ended 1989.

Notes: Srs 10 was initial US domestic version and Srs 30 and long-range Srs 30ER are the principal intercontinental versions, the Srs 40 being similar with switch from CF6 to JT9D engines. *Photo:* DC-10-30F.

McDONNELL DOUGLAS DC-10

Dimensions: Span, 165 ft 4 in (50,40 m); length, 182 ft 1 in (55,50 m); height, 58 ft 1 in (17,7 m); wing area, 3,958 sq ft (367,7 m²).
Weights (Srs 30): Operating weight empty, 267,197 lb (121 198 kg); max payload, 106,550 lb (48 330 kg); max fuel, 245,566 lb (111 387 kg); max zero fuel, 368,000 lb (166 922 kg); max take-off, 572,000 lb (259 450 kg); max landing, 403,000 lb (182 798 kg).

McDONNELL DOUGLAS MD-11

Dimensions: Span, 169 ft 6 in (51,70 m); overall length, 200 ft 10 in (61,21 m); overall height, 57 ft 9 in (17,6 m); wing area, 3,648 sq ft (338,9 m²).

Weights: Operating weight empty, 288,880 lb (132 036 kg); max payload, 112,564 lb (51 060 kg); max fuel, 269,226 lb (122 121 kg); max take-off, 602,500 lb (273 300 kg); optional max take-off weight, 618,000 lb (280 325 kg); max landing, 430,000 lb (195 045 kg); max zero fuel, 400,000 lb (181 437 kg).

McDONNELL DOUGLAS MD-11

Country of Origin: USA.

Type: Very long-range wide-bodied jetliner.

Power Plant: Three 61,500 lb st (273,6 kN) General Electric CF6-80C2-D1F or 60,000 lb st (266,9 kN) Pratt & Whitney PW4460 or 65,000 lb st (289,1 kN) Rolls-Royce Trent 665 turbofans.

Performance: Max cruising speed, Mach = 0.87, 510 kts (945 km/h) at 31,000 ft (9 450 m); economical cruise, 473 kts (876 km/h) at 35,000 ft (10 670 m); range with 323 passengers, 6,785 naut mls (12 566 km); range with 293 passengers (three-class), 6,933 naut mls (12 840 km); max range, 8,232 naut mls (15 250 km).

Accommodation: Flight crew of two. Typical two-class layout for 323 passengers. Max seating for 405, 10-abreast at 32-in (81-cm) seat pitch.

Status: First of five development/certification aircraft flown 10 January 1990 and second on 1 March, both with CF6-80C2 engines. Third aircraft flown 26 April 1990 with PW4460 engines. Fourth and fifth flown during 1990, with CF6-80C2 engines, plus several production delivery standard aircraft. Certification (CF6-80 engines) 8 November 1990, (PW4460) 19 December 1990. First delivery (Finnair) 29 November and entry into service 21 December 1990. First delivery to US operator (Delta, lease from Mitsui) 14 December 1990 for entry into service early 1991. First flight and certification with Trent engines in 1993.

Sales: Total commitments, 377 for 32 customers, including 179 firm orders.

Notes: MD-11 was launched end 1986 after two years of development and market study to define a successor for the DC-10. Basic MD-11 has DC-10 Srs 30 fuselage lengthened by 18 ft 9 in (5,71 m); combi and freighter variants are available. MD-11ER has been proposed with the original DC-10 fuselage length and greater range. Also planned is the MD-12 with 35 ft (10,67 m) more fuselage length and major wing improvements.

NAMC YS-11

Country of Origin: Japan.

Type: Short-range turboprop transport.

Power Plant: Two 3,060 shp (2 282 kW) Rolls-Royce Dart 542-10K turboprops.

Performance (-200): Max cruising speed, 253 kts (469 km/h) at 15,000 ft (4 575 m); best economy cruise, 244 kts (452 km/h) at 20,000 ft (6 100 m); range with max payload (no reserves), 590 naut mls (1 090 km); range with max fuel (no reserves), 1,736 naut mls (3 215 km).

Accommodation: Flight crew of two or three and 60 passengers four-abreast with central aisle at 34-in (86-cm) pitch.

Status: Two prototypes flown on 30 August and 28 December 1962 respectively; first production YS-11 flown 23 October 1964, certification 25 August 1964, entered service (Toa Airways) April 1965. First YS-11A-200 flown 27 November 1967, certificated (by FAA) 3 April 1968. YS-11A-400 flown 17 September 1969. Production completed February 1974.

Sales: Production of the YS-11 totalled 182 (including prototypes), comprising 49 Srs 100, 95 Srs 200, 16 Srs 300, nine Srs 400, four Srs 500 and nine Srs 600; of the total, 23 sold initially to Japanese armed forces and remainder commercial. In early 1991, 103 remained in commercial service, and 41 with military and government agencies.

Notes: The YS-11 was Japan's first post-war commercial transport to enter production, having been designed and built by a consortium made up of Mitsubishi, Kawasaki, Fuji, Shin Meiwa, Japan Aircraft Manufacturing and Showa. The major users in 1990 were the Japanese domestic airlines Japan Air Service and All Nippon, Mid Pacific Airlines in Hawaii and Airborne Express in the US. *Photo:* YS-11A.

NAMC YS-11A

Dimensions: Span, 104 ft 11¾ in (32,00 m); length 86 ft 3½ in (26,30 m); height, 29 ft 5½ in (8,98 m); wing area, 1,020.4 sq ft (94,8 m²).
Weights (-200): Operating weight empty, 33,993 lb (15 419 kg); max payload, 14,508 lb (6 581 kg); max fuel, 12,830 lb (5 820 kg); max zero fuel, 48,500 lb (22 000 kg); max take-off, 54,010 lb (24 500 kg); max landing, 52,910 lb (24 000 kg).

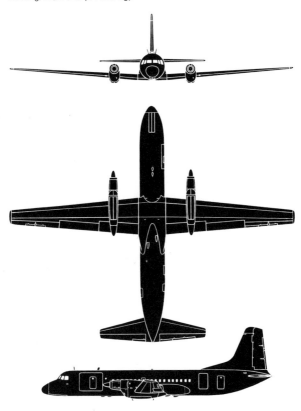

SAAB 340

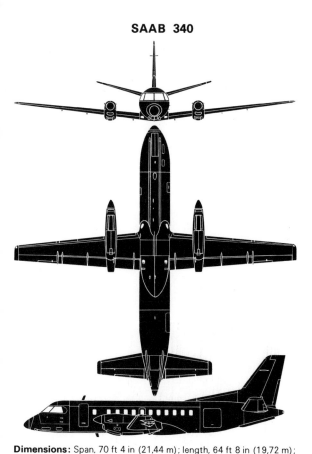

Dimensions: Span, 70 ft 4 in (21,44 m); length, 64 ft 8 in (19,72 m); height, 22 ft 6 in (6,87 m); wing area, 450 sq ft (41,80 m²).
Weights: Operating weight empty, 17,715 lb (8 035 kg); max payload, 8,285 lb (3 758 kg); max fuel, 5,690 lb (2 581 kg); max take-off, 28,500 lb (12 927 kg); max landing, 28,000 lb (12 701 kg); max zero fuel, 26,000 lb (11 794 kg).

SAAB 340

Country of Origin: Sweden.
Type: Regional airliner.
Power Plant: Two 1,735 eshp (1 294 kW) General Electric CT7-5A2 or (340B) 1,870 shp (1 394 kW) CT7-9B turboprops.
Performance: Max cruise, 282 kts (522 km/h) at 15,000 ft (4 570 m); economical cruise, 264 kts (489 km/h) at 25,000 ft (7 620 m); range with max payload, 643 naut mls (1 191 km); range with max fuel, 1,848 naut mls (3 422 km).
Accommodation: Flight crew of two and 35 passengers at 30-in (76-cm) pitch three-abreast with offset aisle. Max seating for 37.
Status: Three prototypes flown on 25 January, 11 May and 25 August 1983 respectively; first full production standard aircraft flown 5 March 1984. Certification 30 May 1984, first delivery (Crossair) 6 June and first revenue service 14 June 1984. Flight testing of Saab 340B features (in second prototype 340) began September 1987. First 340B delivered (Crossair) 15 September 1989.
Sales: Total 330 sold (plus options) by February 1991. First 160 were Saab 340A, thereafter Saab 340B.
Notes: Saab-Scania and Fairchild concluded an agreement on 25 January 1980, to develop the Model 340 regional airliner on a 50–50 basis. At the end of 1985, Fairchild withdrew from the SF-340 programme and Saab-Scania assumed full responsibility for marketing, with wing construction transferred to Sweden in 1987. Saab 340B (details above) switched from 1,735 shp (1 294 kW) CT7-5A2 engines and introduced an extended span tailplane. *Photo:* Saab 340A.

SAAB 2000

Country of Origin: Sweden.
Type: Short-haul regional airliner.
Power Plant: Two Allison GMA 2100 turboprops each rated at 3,285 shp (2 451 kW) for take-off and at 3,650 shp (2 724 kW) with automatic power reserve (APR).
Performance: Max cruising speed, 360 kts (667 km/h); range with max payload, 750 naut mls (1 390 km); range with max fuel, 1,400 naut mls (2 593 km).
Accommodation: Flight crew of two. Typical layout for 50 passengers, three-abreast. Max seating for 58, three-abreast at 30-in (76-cm) seat pitch.
Status: Final definition and marketing launch in late 1988. First flight, first quarter 1992; certification and first delivery second half 1993.
Sales: Total orders and options, 189 by January 1991, for more than six customers. Launch order for 25 (plus 25 options) placed by Crossair; three other customers ordered 16 (plus 5 options) and 64 more options held by three other airlines.
Notes: The Saab 2000 evolved from extensive studies of possible stretched derivatives of the Saab 340 (see previous entry). It has the same fuselage cross section and same basic wing structure, but a lengthened fuselage and increased wing span. Emphasis placed on cruising speed and high initial rate of climb allows Saab to claim that the 2000 will compete in performance with forthcoming regional jets, whilst offering greater economy of operation. Saab has arranged for CASA in Spain to complete detailed design and undertake production of the entire wing of the Saab 2000. Valmet in Finland is responsible for the vertical and horizontal tail surfaces and Westland in the UK manufactures the rear fuselage, leaving Saab responsible for the remainder of the fuselage and for assembly, installation of systems and equipment, and flight testing.

SAAB 2000

Dimensions: Span, 81 ft 3 in (24,76 m); overall length, 88 ft 8 in (27,03 m); overall height, 25 ft 4 in (7,73 m); wing area, 600 sq ft (55,74 m²).

Weights: Operating weight empty, 28,000 lb (12 700 kg); max payload, 13,000 lb (5 900 kg); max fuel, 9,180 lb (4 165 kg); max take-off, 47,000 lb (21 320 kg); max landing, 45,000 lb (20 410 kg); max zero fuel, 41,000 lb (18 600 kg).

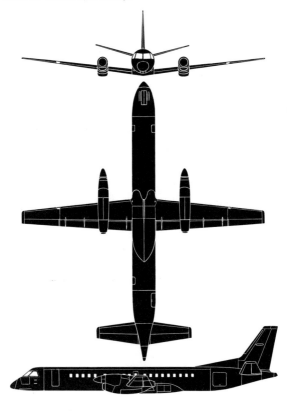

SHORTS 330

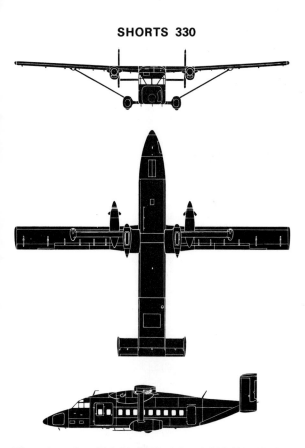

Dimensions: Span, 74 ft 8 in (22,76 m); length, 58 ft 0½ in (17,69 m); height, 16 ft 3 in (4,95 m); wing area, 453 sq ft (42,10 m²).
Weights (330-200): Operating weight empty, 14,764 lb (6 697 kg); max payload (passenger), 5,850 lb (2 655 kg); max payload (freight), 7,500 lb (3 400 kg); max fuel, 4,480 lb (2 032 kg); max take-off, 22,900 lb (10 387 kg), max landing, 22,600 lb (10 251 kg).

SHORTS 330

Country of Origin: United Kingdom.
Type: Regional airliner.
Power Plant: Two (330–100) 1,173 shp (875 kW) Pratt & Whitney PT6A-45A or PT6A-45B or (330–200) 1,198 shp (893 kW) PT6A-45R turboprops.
Performance (330–200): Max cruise, 190 kts (352 km/h) at 10,000 ft (3 050 m); long-range cruise, 159 kts (294 km/h) at 10,000 ft (3 050 m); max payload range, (no reserves), 473 naut mls (660 km); range with max fuel, (no reserves) 915 naut mls (1 695 km).
Accommodation: Flight crew of two and 30 passengers at 30-in (76-cm) pitch three-abreast with offset aisle.
Status: Engineering prototypes (SD3-30) flown on 22 August 1974, with production prototype following on 8 July 1975. First production aircraft flown 15 December 1975, first customer deliveries mid-1976, entry into service (Time Air, Canada) 24 August 1976.
Sales: Approximately 190 examples of Shorts 330 sold, including military (Sherpa and C-23) models.
Notes: As the SD3-30, the Shorts 330 was evolved from the Skyvan, with same fuselage cross section but lengthened, and with greater wing span. Original gross weight was 22,690 lb (10 250 kg) with PT6A-45 engines. The 330-200 incorporates a number of product improvements, having similar engines to those of the 360 (see next entry), permitting elimination of the water-methanol system of the -100 and featuring as standard several items previously listed as options. The name Sherpa is used for a version with rear-loading door, first flown 23 December 1982.

SHORTS 360

Country of Origin: United Kingdom.
Type: Regional airliner.
Power Plant: Two flat-rated 1,424 shp (1 063 kW) Pratt & Whitney PT6A-65AR turboprops.
Performance: Max cruise, 212 kts (393 km/h) at 10,000 ft (3 050 m); long-range cruise, 180 kts (333 km/h) at 10,000 ft (3 050 m); max payload range (36 passengers) (no reserves), 225 naut mls (417 km); range with max fuel, 861 naut mls (1 595 km).
Accommodation: Flight crew of two and 36 passengers at 30-in (76-cm) pitch three-abreast with offset aisle.
Status: Prototype first flown on 1 June 1981; first production 360 flown 19 August 1982 with certification on 3 September, and first customer delivery on 11 November 1982 (to Suburban Airlines of Pennsylvania) following US certification. First 360-300 delivery (to Philippine Airlines) 18 March 1987.
Sales: Total of 181 sold by end of 1990.
Notes: Essentially a growth version of the Shorts 330 (see previous entry) the 360 differs from its progenitor primarily in having a 3-ft (91-cm) cabin stretch ahead of the wing and an entirely redesigned rear fuselage and tail assembly. These changes allow cabin capacity to be increased by two seat rows and result in lower aerodynamic drag which contributes to a higher performance. Like the 330, the 360 is unpressurized. Early aircraft had lower-rated PT6A-65R engines, the PT6A-65AR being introduced in November 1985 in the Shorts 360-300, which also featured six-bladed propellers.

SHORTS 360

Dimensions: Span, 74 ft 10 in (22,81 m); length, 70 ft 10 in (21,59 m); height, 23 ft 10 in (7,27 m); wing area, 453 sq ft (42,10 m²).
Weights: Operating weight empty, 17,350 lb (7 870 kg); max payload, 7,020 lb (3 184 kg); max fuel, 3,840 lb (1 741 kg); max take-off, 27,100 lb (12 292 kg); max landing, 26,500 lb (12 020 kg).

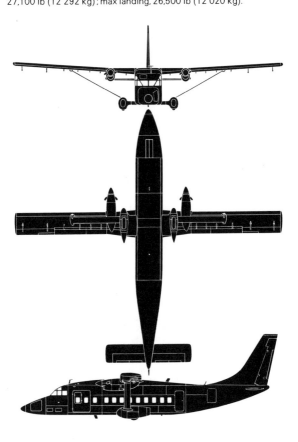

TUPOLEV TU-134

Dimensions: Span, 95 ft 1¾ in (29,00 m); length, 121 ft 6½ in (37,05 m); height, 30 ft 0 in (9,14 m); wing area, 1,370.3 sq ft (127,3 m²).
Weights: Operating weight empty, 64,045 lb (29 050 kg); max payload, 18,075 lb (8 200 kg); max fuel weight, 31,800 lb (14 400 kg); max take-off, 103,600 lb (47 000 kg); max landing, 94,800 lb (43 000 kg).

TUPOLEV TU-134A

Country of Origin: Soviet Union.
Type: Short-medium-range jetliner.
Power Plant: Two 14,990 lb st (66,7 kN) Soloviev D-30 Srs II turbofans.
Performance (Tu-134A): Max cruise, 486 kts (898 km/h) at 28,000 ft (8 500 m); long-range cruise, 405 kts (750 km/h); range with max payload, 1,020 naut mls (1 890 km); range with payload of 11,025 lb (5 000 kg), 1,630 naut mls (3 020 km).
Accommodation: Flight crew of three (two pilots and a navigator). Max one-class layout, 84 passengers; typical mixed class accommodation, 12F plus 54E, all four-abreast with central aisle.
Status: Prototype testing began late 1962, with five more aircraft flown 1963/64. Full commercial service began (with Aeroflot) September 1967 on Moscow–Stockholm route. Tu-134A entered service 1970.
Sales: More than 700 built for Aeroflot and for export to the East European airlines and Yugoslavia.
Notes: The Tu-134 emerged at about the same time as such Western types as the BAC One-Eleven and McDonnell Douglas DC-9, with which it shared a similar rear-engined T-tailed layout, and was the Tupolev design bureau's first wholly-original design for commercial use. The Tu-134A differs from the original model in having the fuselage lengthened by 6 ft 10½ in (2,10 m) and improved equipment. The Tu-134B has a forward-facing crew compartment. The Tu-134B-1 has a revised interior for up to 90 passengers (without a galley) and the Tu-134B-3, with D-30-III turbofans, can seat 96 with full toilet and galley facilities retained. The Tu-134OK designation refers to a proposed version with cryogenic fuel. *Photo:* Tu-134B-3.

TUPOLEV TU-154

Country of Origin: Soviet Union.
Type: Medium-range jetliner.
Power Plant: Three (Tu-154) 20,950 lb st (93,2 kN) Kuznetsov NK-8-2 or (Tu-154A and B) 23,150 lb st (103 kN) NK-8-2U or (Tu-154M) 23,380 lb st (104 kN) Soloviev D-30KU-154-II turbofans.
Performance (Tu-154M): Typical cruising speed, 513 kts (950 km/h) at 39,000 ft (11 900 m); range with max payload, 2,100 naut mls (3 900 km); range with 12,015-lb (5 450-kg) payload, 3,563 naut mls (6 600 km).
Accommodation: Flight crew of three or four; typical mixed-class layout for 154 passengers; maximum 180 six-abreast at 29.5-in (75-cm) pitch.
Status: First of six prototype/development Tu-154s flown on 4 October 1968. First commercial service by Aeroflot 9 February 1972, and first international service (Moscow–Prague) 1 August 1972. First Tu-154Ms delivered 27 December 1984.
Sales: Some 700 Tu-154, A and B, delivered to Aeroflot and for export. Tu-154M remains in production in 1990.
Notes: Original Tu-154A was succeeded in 1977 by Tu-154B and Tu-154B-2 with higher weights, improved systems, etc. Tu-154C is an all-cargo variant. Tu-154M with Soloviev in place of Kuznetsov engines also has redesigned tailplane, smaller wing slats and larger spoilers. Tu-155 designation applies to a Tu-154 modified as test-bed for NK-88 engine (centre installation only) using cryogenic fuels, leading to the proposed Tu-156 with three NK-89s. *Photo:* Tu-154M.

TUPOLEV TU-154

Dimensions: Span, 123 ft 2½ in (37,55 m); length, 157 ft 1¾ in (47,90 m); height, 37 ft 4¾ in (11,40 m); wing area, 2,169 sq ft (201,45 m²).

Weights (Tu-154M): Basic operating, 121,915 lb (55 300 kg); max payload, 39,680 lb (18 000 kg); max fuel load, 87,633 lb (39 750 kg); max zero fuel weight, 163,140 lb (74 000 kg); max take-off, 220,460 lb (100 000 kg).

TUPOLEV TU-204

Dimensions: Span, 137 ft 9½ in (42,00 m); length, 151 ft 7¾ in (46,22 m); height, 45 ft 6½ in (13,88 m); gross wing area, 1,982.5 sq ft (184,17 m²).

Weights: Operating weight empty, 124,560 lb (56 500 kg); max fuel, 52,910 lb (24 000 kg); max payload, 46,300 lb (21 000 kg); max take-off, 206,125 lb (93 500 kg); max landing, 189,595 lb (86 000 kg); max zero fuel, 170,855 lb (77 500 kg).

TUPOLEV TU-204

Country of Origin: Soviet Union.

Type: Medium-range jetliner.

Power Plant: Two Soloviev (Perm) PS-90A turbofans each rated at 35,275 lb st (156,9 kN) for take-off.

Performance: Max cruise, 458 kts (850 km/h) at 35,000 ft (10 650 m); economical cruise, 437 kts (810 km/h) at 40,000 ft (12 200 m); range with payload of 41,887 lb (19 000 kg), 2,077 naut mls (3 850 km).

Accommodation: Flight crew of two pilots and (optional) flight engineer. Typical two-class layout for 12F (four-abreast) and 184E passengers, six-abreast with single aisle. Max passengers, 214, six-abreast, at 32-in (81-cm) pitch.

Status: Prototype first flown on 2 January 1989. Second prototype and first production aircraft (from Ulyanovsk assembly line) flown in 1990. Production initiated for Aeroflot.

Sales: Aeroflot requirement for 350-500, with entry into service planned for 1992.

Notes: Tu-204 is Soviet counterpart of the Boeing 757, with similar twin-engined configuration and long, single-aisle cabin layout. Advanced construction and materials are matched by modern technology systems, with triplicated fly-by-wire digital flight controls and dual EFIS, six-CRT display flight deck, arranged to permit two-pilot operation if required. Flight control system has no mechanical back-up for the FBW controls, but a three-channel analogue back-up system takes over automatically if two of the digital channels fail. The system provides for full Cat IIIA operation when fully developed. Planned production embraces the initial Tu-204-100 at 219,355 lb (99 500 kg) with a full passenger range of 2,860 naut mls (5 300 km), and the Tu-204-200 at 239,200 lb (108 500 kg) with extra fuel for a range of 3,875 naut mls (7 180 km). Tupolev has chosen the Rolls-Royce RB211-535 to power the Tu-204-200, in the 40,550 lb st (180,4 kN) E5 or 43,600 lb st (194 kN) F5 versions of the engine.

VICKERS VISCOUNT

Country of Origin: United Kingdom.
Type: Short-range turboprop transport.
Power Plant: Four 2,100 ehp (1 566 kW) Rolls-Royce Dart 525 turboprops.
Performance (V.810): Typical cruising speed, 304 kts (563 km/h) at 20,000 ft (6 100 m); range with max (64-passenger) payload, 843 naut mls (1 560 km); range with max fuel, 877 naut mls (1 625 km).
Accommodation: Flight crew of two or three and up to 69 passengers five-abreast with off-set aisle, at 34-in (86-cm) pitch.
Status: V.630 prototype for Viscount series first flown 16 July 1948; V.700 flown 19 April 1950; first production V.701 flown 20 August 1952, certificated 17 April 1953 and entered service (BEA) 18 April. V.800 prototype flown 27 July 1956, first delivery (V.802 for BEA) 11 January 1957. V.810 prototype flown 23 December 1957. Production completed 1964.
Sales: Total of 438 Viscounts sold, plus six prototypes and unsold demonstrators. Major fleet buyers were BEA, TCA and Capital Airlines, About 30 Viscounts in airline service in 1991, plus others as executive transports.
Notes: The Viscount was the world's first turboprop airliner, entering service almost a year after the de Havilland Comet had become the world's first turbojet transport. The Viscount was also to prove the best-selling commercial transport of all-British design and production. The V.700 and V.800 variants differ in fuselage length, power and weights; individual customer variants within each series had identifying designations with '7' or '8' prefixes as appropriate. *Photo:* V.802.

VICKERS VISCOUNT

Dimensions (V.810): Span, 93 ft 8½ in (28,50 m); length, 85 ft 8 in (26,11 m); height, 26 ft 9 in (8,16 m); wing area, 963 sq ft (89,46 m²).
Weights (V.810): Basic operating, 41,565 lb (18 753 kg); max payload, 14,500 lb (6 577 kg); max fuel weight, 15,609 lb (7 080 kg); max zero fuel, 57,500 lb (26 082 kg); max take-off, 72,500 lb (32 886 kg); max landing, 62,000 lb (28 123 kg).

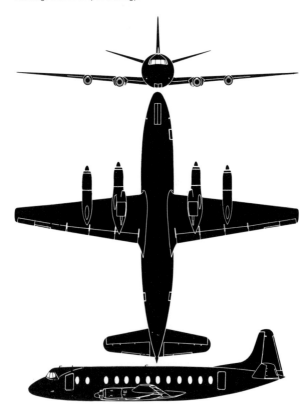

XIAN Y7-100

Dimensions: Span, 97 ft 3 in (29,64 m); length, 77 ft 9 in (23,70 m); height, 28 ft 0½ in (8,55 m); wing area, 807.1 sq ft (74,98 m²).
Weights: Operating weight empty, 32,850 lb (14 900 kg); max payload, 12,125 lb (5 500 kg); max fuel, 10,560 lb (4 790 kg); max zero fuel, 43,332 lb (19 655 kg); max take-off, 48,060 lb (21 800 kg); max landing, 48,060 lb (21 800 kg).

XIAN Y7-100

Country of Origin: China.

Type: Short-to-medium-range regional turboprop transport.

Power Plant: Two 2,550 shp (1 901 kW) Shanghai Wojiang WJ-5A-1 turboprops.

Performance: Max cruising speed, 261 kts (484 km/h) at 13,125 ft (4 000 m); long-range cruising speed, 228 kts (423 km/h) at 19,685 ft (6 000 m); range with full 52-passenger payload, 490 naut mls (910 km); range with standard fuel, 1,026 naut mls (1 900 km); range with max and auxiliary fuel, 1,305 naut mls (2 420 km).

Accommodation: Flight crew of three and up to 52 passengers four-abreast with central aisle.

Status: Prototype Y7-100 flown in Hong Kong autumn 1985. First production Y7-100 flown late 1986.

Sales: Total of 40 in production for delivery to Chinese regional airlines, nearing completion in 1991.

Notes: After receiving a substantial number of Antonov An-24 transports from the Soviet Union, China has developed its own production drawings to allow manufacture of the type at the Xian factory. A pre-production example of the Chinese-built version, known as the Y7, was displayed in April 1982 and the first flight of a production Y7 was reported on 1 February 1984, with delivery to CAAC soon after. During 1985, Hong Kong Aircraft Engineering Co developed the Y7-100 featuring a revised and modernized cockpit, improved cabin, systems and avionics using Western equipment, and winglets. The Y7-200A and -200B, developed with assistance from Boeing, feature improvements to give better operating economy. The Y7-500 is a cargo version with An-26 style rear ramp.

YAKOVLEV YAK-40

Country of Origin: Soviet Union.
Type: Regional airliner.
Power Plant: Three 3,300 lb st (1 500 kgp) Ivchenko AI-25 turbofan engines.
Performance: Max cruising speed, 297 kts (550 km/h); range with max payload (32 passengers), 782 naut mls (1 450 km); range with max fuel, 971 naut mls (1 800 km).
Accommodation: Flight crew of two, with provision for third man on flight deck. Standard layout for 27 passengers three-abreast with offset aisle, at pitch of 29.7 in (77,5 cm); maximum high-density seating 32, four-abreast at same pitch.
Status: Prototype first flown 21 October 1966. Entered service with Aeroflot 30 September 1968. Production (commercial and military) complete.
Sales: Approximately 1,000 built, principally for use by Aeroflot. Some exports to companies or governments in Italy, Federal Germany, Afghanistan, Angola, Czechoslovakia, Bulgaria, Vietnam, and Yugoslavia.
Notes: Yakovlev's first jet transport, the Yak-40 was designed to meet Soviet needs for a short-haul transport of modest capacity, to replace piston-engined Il-12s and Il-14s, and even older Li-2s. It flies on scheduled services but is also used for ambulance and air taxi duties and several have been supplied for military use. An effort was also made to adapt the Yak-40 for the US commuter airline market, by fitting Garrett TFE731 turbofans and Collins avionics; this programme was handled by ICX Aviation as the X-Avia, but it did not proceed. An all-freight version of the Yak-40 is used in the Soviet Union, where more than 700 were reported to be still in service in 1990.

YAKOVLEV YAK-40

Dimensions: Span, 82 ft 0¼ in (25,00 m); length, 66 ft 9½ in (20,36 m); height, 21 ft 4 in (6,50 m); wing area, 735.5 sq ft (70,0 m²).
Weights: Empty weight, 20,725 lb (9 400 kg); max payload, 5,070 lb (2 300 kg); max fuel load, 8,820 lb (4 000 kg); max take-off weight, 35,275 lb (16 000 kg).

YAKOVLEV YAK-42

Dimensions: Span, 114 ft 5¼ in (34,88 m); length, 119 ft 4¼ in (36,38 m); height, 32 ft 3 in (9,83 m); wing area, 1,615 sq ft (150 m²).
Weights: Empty weight, 76,236 lb (34 580 kg); max payload, 28,220 lb (12 800 kg); max fuel load, 40,785 lb (18 500 kg); max take-off, 124,560 lb (56 500 kg); max landing, 111,333 lb (50 500 kg).

YAKOVLEV YAK-42

Country of Origin: Soviet Union.

Type: Short-medium-range jetliner.

Power Plant: Three 14,330 lb st (63,74 kN) Lotarev D-36 turbofans.

Performance: Max cruising speed, 437 kts (810 km/h) at 25,000 ft (7 600 m); best economy cruise, 400 kts (740 km/h); range with max payload, 700 naut mls (1 300 km) at 400 kts (740 km/h) at 29,500 ft (9 000 m); range with max passenger payload, 1,025 naut mls (1 900 km).

Accommodation: Flight crew of two. Standard arrangement (Yak-42D) for 120 passengers six-abreast with central aisle, at 29.5-in (75-cm) pitch.

Status: First of three prototypes flown 7 March 1975. First production aircraft flown 1980, and Aeroflot services began at the end of that year, on Moscow–Krasnodar route. In production.

Sales: About 100 built for service with Aeroflot by 1990, from initial planned batch of 200. First export sales of Yak-42D to China (10) and Cuba (4) announced early 1990, and first deliveries outside the Soviet area of influence expected in 1991, to an operator in Italy.

Notes: The Yak-42 was developed primarily to replace the Tu-134 on Aeroflot's domestic routes. The first prototype had only 11 deg of wing sweepback but subsequent prototypes and the production aircraft have 23 deg of sweepback and production Yak-42s differ from prototypes in having four-wheeled main landing gear bogies. The Yak-42D, introduced in 1990, featured increased wing fuel capacity, systems improvements and gross weight increased from 119,000 lb (54 000 kg) to 124,560 lb (56 500 kg). A 'stretched' 140-seat version, the Yak-42M, is reported to be under development with 16,550 lb st (73,6 kN) D-436 turbofans, and the Yak-46 is a derivative design under study with a pair of aft-mounted D-27 propfans or underwing high by-pass turbofans.

AERO SPACELINES GUPPY 201

Country of Origin: USA.

Power Plant: Four 4,912 ehp (3 666 kW) Allison 501-D22C turbo-props.

Dimensions: Span, 156 ft 3 in (47,62 m); overall length, 143 ft 10 in (43,84 m); overall height, 48 ft 6 in (14,78 m); gross wing area, 1,965 sq ft (182,5 m²).

Weights: Operating weight empty, 100,000 lb (45 360 kg); max payload, 54,000 lb (24 494 kg); max take-off, 170,000 lb (77 100 kg); max landing, 160,000 lb (72 570 kg); max zero fuel, 154,000 lb (69 854 kg).

Performance: Max cruise, 250 kts (463 km/h) at 20,000 ft (6 100 m); economical cruise, 220 kts (407 km/h) at 20,000 ft (6 100 m); range with max payload, 440 naut mls (813 km); range with max fuel, 2,540 naut mls (4 700 km).

Accommodation: Flight crew of four.

Status: First two Super Guppy 201 conversions flown in US on 24 August 1970 and 24 August 1971. Aircraft Nos 3 and 4 flown in France on 11 June 1982 and 2 August 1983.

Sales: Four conversions only, acquired by Airbus Industries.

Notes: The unique Guppy family of aircraft was conceived by the late John Conroy, starting with the massive Pregnant Guppy conversion of a Boeing Stratocruiser, flown on 19 September 1962. The Super Guppy in 1965 was even larger and led to the Super Guppy 201 which added Allison turboprops to the outsize fuselage with hinged nose for straight-in loading of outsize items. These two aircraft, and two similar conversions made by UTA in France, are operated exclusively by Airbus to ferry fuselage components and wings between the production centres and assembly lines in Europe.

175

ANTONOV AN-12

Country of Origin: Soviet Union.
Power Plant: Four 3,945 shp (2 942 kW) Ivchenko AI-20K turbo-props.
Dimensions: Span, 124 ft 8 in (38,00 m); length, 108 ft 7¼ in (33,10 m); height, 34 ft 6½ in (10,53 m); wing area, 1,310 sq ft (121,70 m²).
Weights (military freighter): Empty, about 61,730 lb (28 000 kg); max payload, 44,090 lb (20 000 kg); normal take-off, 121,475 lb (55 100 kg); max take-off, 134,480 lb (61 000 kg).
Performance: Max cruising speed, 361 kts (670 km/h); range with max payload, 1,940 naut mls (3 600 km); range with max fuel, 3,075 naut mls (5 700 km).
Accommodation: Flight crew of five (two pilots, radio operator, flight engineer and navigator). Normally operates only as a freighter, with a pressurized compartment for 14 passengers.
Status: First flown 1958 (approx) and entered military service in 1959. Out of production.
Sales: Approximately 900 An-12s built (for all purposes, including military). About 200 in Aeroflot service in 1990.
Notes: The An-12 was evolved to meet specific Soviet needs for a military transport, based on the An-10 which was one of the first

---

ANTONOV AN-22 ANTHEUS

Country of Origin: Soviet Union.
Power Plant: Four 15,000 shp (11 186 kW) Kuznetsov NK-12MA turboprops.
Dimensions: Span, 211 ft 4 in (64,40 m); length, approximately 190 ft 0 in (57,92 m); height, 41 ft 1½ in (12,53 m); wing area, 3,713 sq ft (345 m²).
Weights: Typical empty, equipped, 251,325 lb (114 000 kg); max payload, 176,350 lb (80 000 kg); max fuel load, 94,800 lb (43 000 kg); max take-off, 551,160 lb (250 000 kg).
Performance: Max level speed, 399 kts (740 km/h); range with max payload, 2,690 naut mls (5 000 km); range with max fuel, carrying a payload of 99,200 lb (45 000 kg), 5,900 naut mls (10 950 km).
Accommodation: Flight crew of five or six, including two pilots, flight engineer, navigator and communications engineer. Standard layout includes a compartment for 28–29 passengers behind the flight deck.
Status: Prototype first flown on 27 February 1965. Pre-production aircraft used on Aeroflot proving flights 1967. Out of production.
Sales: Used only by Aeroflot and Soviet military services. About 70 built.

turboprop-powered airliners put into service by Aeroflot. A sizeable number is operated in 'civil' guise by Aeroflot for freight carrying and others supplied to foreign governments similarly operate in airline markings on quasi-commercial duties.

Notes: Approximately 50 An-22s are known to have operated in Aeroflot markings, frequently being engaged in ferrying military supplies and personnel around the world, the use of 'civil' aircraft in such cases facilitating overflights and transits through foreign countries.

ANTONOV AN-72 and AN-74

Country of Origin: Soviet Union.

Power Plant (An-72A): Two 14,330 lb st (6 500 kgp) Lotarev D-36 turbofans.

Dimensions: Span, 104 ft 7½ in (31,89 m); overall length, 92 ft 1¼ in (28,07 m); overall height, 28 ft 4½ in (8,65 m); gross wing area, 1,062 sq ft (98,62 m²).

Weights: Max payload, 22,045 lb (10 000 kg); max take-off, 76,060 lb (34 500 kg); max STOL take-off, 3,280-ft/1000-m runway, 60,625 lb (27 500 kg).

Performance (An-72A): Max speed, 380 kts (705 km/h) at 32,800 ft (10 000 m); economical cruise, 300 kts (556 km/h) at 32,800 ft (10 000 m); range with max payload, 430 naut mls (800 km); range with max fuel, 2,590 naut mls (4 800 km).

Accommodation: Flight crew of three (two pilots and flight engineer). An-74 has crew of five including navigator and radio operator.

Status: First of two prototypes flown 22 December 1977. Eight pre-production examples preceded An-72A production.

Sales: Production exclusively for Aeroflot and Soviet military use.

Notes: The An-72 is unique, as a production aircraft, in that it features upper surface blowing, a means of increasing lift by use of the Coanda effect, achieved by discharging the engine exhaust directly over the upper wing surface, and using large-area trailing-edge flaps. With its rear loading ramp and cabin adapted for freight carrying, the An-72 is intended primarily for cargo-carrying but can accommodate up to 68 passengers. It also has military applications. The An-74, of the same overall configuration, is equipped for all-weather operations in the Polar regions, with an optional wheel/ski undercarriage. *Photo:* An-74.

ANTONOV AN-124

Country of Origin: Soviet Union.

Power Plant: Four 51,650 lb st (23 430 kgp) Lotarev D-18T turbofans.

Dimensions: Span, 240 ft 5¾ in (73,30 m); length, 226 ft 8½ in (69,10 m); height, 68 ft 2¼ in (20,78 m); wing area, 6,760 sq ft (628,0 m²).

Weights: Max payload, 330,700 lb (150 000 kg); max fuel, 507,063 lb (230 000 kg); max take-off, 892,872 lb (405 000 kg).

Performance: Max cruising speed, 467 kts (865 km/h); long-range cruising speed, 432–459 kts (800–850 km/h) at 32,800–39,370 ft (10 000–12 000 m); range with max payload, 2,430 naut mls (4 500 km); range with max fuel, 8,900 naut mls (16 500 km).

Accommodation: Flight crew of four. Up to 88 passengers on upper deck aft of flight deck.

Status: Prototype first flight on 26 December 1982. Entered service, January 1986.

Sales: Production exclusively for Aeroflot and Soviet military forces. About 40 built.

Notes: Aerodynamically conventional, the An-124 was the world's largest aircraft when it first appeared, but has now been superceded by the six-engined An-225. It makes extensive use of composites in its structure, and has a fly-by-wire control system. The 24-wheel undercarriage, including four nosewheels, allows the An-124 to operate from relatively unprepared surfaces such as hard-packed snow and ice-covered swampland. The fuselage axis can also be adjusted, up or down, to facilitate loading through the nose door or rear ramp. Primarily a military strategic freighter, the An-124 is also seen operating in Aeroflot colours and in 1990 two examples became available for world-wide cargo charter flying, through the UK-based Air Foyle company.

CANADAIR CL-44

Country of Origin: Canada.

Power Plant: Four 5,730 shp (4 276 kW) Rolls-Royce Tyne 515/10 turboprops.

Dimensions: Span, 142 ft 3½ in (43,37 m); length, 136 ft 10¾ in (41,73 m); height, 38 ft 9 in (11,80 m); wing area, 2,075 sq ft (192,72 m²).

Weights: Operating weight empty, 88,952 lb (40 345 kg); max payload, 66,048 lb (29 959 kg); max fuel, 81,448 lb (36 944 kg); max zero fuel, 155,000 lb (70 308 kg); max take-off, 210,000 lb (95 250 kg); max landing, 165,000 lb (74 843 kg).

Performance: Max cruising speed, 349 kts (647 km/h) at 20,000 ft (6 100 m); range with max payload, 2,850 naut mls (5 300 km); range with max fuel and 35,564-lb (16 132-kg) payload, 4,850 naut mls (8 990 km).

Accommodation: Flight crew of three.

Status: First CL-44D (military CC-106) flown 15 November 1959; first CL-44D-D (commercial prototype) flown 16 November 1960; first delivery (Flying Tiger) 31 May 1961. CL-44J prototype flown 8 November 1965, CL-44-O conversion flown 26 November 1969.

Sales: Total of 27 CL-44D-4s built.

Notes: Original CL-44D was a Canadian development from the Bristol Britannia design, with lengthened fuselage, greater wing span and new engines. Twelve were built for the RCAF as CC-106 Yukons, several passing into commercial service as freighters when retired in 1973. The CL-44D-4 was built primarily as a commercial freighter, featuring a swing-tail for straight-in loading. The sole CL-44-O has an enlarged diameter upper deck. Less than a dozen CL-44Ds and Yukons were still in airline service, as freighters, in 1990.

CESSNA CARAVAN I

Country of Origin: USA.

Power Plant: One 600 shp (447 kW) Pratt & Whitney PT6A-114 turboprop.

Dimensions: Span, 52 ft 1 in (15,88 m); length, 37 ft 7 in (11,46 m); height, 14 ft 2 in (4,32 m); wing area, 279.4 sq ft (25,96 m²).

Weights: Operating weight empty, 3,800 lb (1 724 kg); max payload, 3,000 lb (1 361 kg); max fuel, 2,224 lb (1 009 kg); max take-off, 7,300 lb (3 311 kg); max landing, 7,300 lb (3 311 kg).

Performance: Max cruising speed, 184 kts (341 km/h) at 10,000 ft (3 050 m); range with max fuel, 1,370 naut mls (2 539 km) at 20,000 ft (6 100 m).

Accommodation: Flight crew of one (and up to nine passengers).

Status: Prototype first flown 9 December 1982. FAA Type Approval 23 October 1984. Deliveries of Model 208A began early 1985. Model 208B first flown 3 March 1986, certificated 9 October and first delivered 31 October 1986.

Sales: Total of about 350 firm sales by early 1991.

Notes: The Caravan was designed by Cessna to provide a light, general utility aircraft, primarily for commercial use carrying assorted loads, but also readily adaptable to a variety of other rôles such as casualty evacuation, para-dropping of supplies or personnel, fire-fighting, aero-surveying, agricultural spraying and so on. A significant market for the type emerged with Federal Express, a specialist company in the overnight delivery of small packages, which has to date bought some 200 Caravan Is in the specially-equipped, windowless Model 208A and 208B versions, known as Cargomaster and Super Cargomaster. The latter has a 4-ft (1,22-m) fuselage 'stretch' and both carry under-fuselage cargo panniers. A passenger-carrying version of the Super Cargomaster is known as the Grand Caravan and seats 14 plus a pilot. Both the extended variants are powered by the 675 shp (504 kW) PT6A-114A engine. *Photo:* Super Cargomaster.

CURTISS C-46

Country of Origin: USA.

Power Plant: Two 2,000 hp (1 496 kW) Pratt & Whitney R-2800-34 piston radial engines.

Dimensions: Span, 108 ft 0 in (32,92 m); overall length, 76 ft 4 in (23,27 m); overall height, 21 ft 8 in (6,60 m); gross wing area, 1,358 sq ft (126,2 m²).

Weights: Operating weight empty, 33,000 lb (14 970 kg); max fuel, 8,400 lb (3 810 kg); max payload, 11,630 lb (85 265 kg); max take-off, 48,000 lb (21 772 kg); max landing, 46,800 lb (21 228 kg); max zero fuel, 45,168 lb (20 488 kg).

Performance: Typical cruise, 162 kts (301 km/h) at 7,000 ft (2 135 m); range with max payload, 96 naut mls (117 km); range with max fuel, 1,017 naut mls (1 880 km) with 5,700-lb (2 585-kg) payload.

Accommodation: Flight crew of two or three.

Status: Prototype Curtiss CW-20 first flown on 26 March 1940. Production total 3,141 for US military use during World War II, under the C-46 designation.

Sales: Several hundred ex-military C-46s 'civilianized' for airline use post-war.

Notes: Small number of ex-military C-46s were used to fly passenger services in the early post-war years but the majority became 'aerial tramps', especially in Central and South America, carrying freight in their capacious fuselages. By 1990, the numbers still flying in this capacity had dwindled to 30 or so.

DOUGLAS DC-6 (and DC-7)

Country of Origin: USA.

Power Plant: Four 2,400 hp (1 790 kW) Pratt & Whitney R-2800-CA-15 air-cooled radial engines.

Dimensions: Span, 117 ft 6 in (35,81 m); length, 105 ft 7 in (32,2 m); height, 29 ft 3 in (8,92 m); wing area, 1,463 sq ft (135,9 m²).

Weights: Operating weight empty, about 62,000 lb (28 123 kg); max payload, 24,565 lb (11 143 kg); max fuel, 32,950 lb (14 946 kg); max zero fuel, 83,200 lb (37 740 kg); max take-off, 107,000 lb (48 534 kg); max landing, 88,200 lb (40 007 kg).

Performance: Max cruising speed, 275 kts (509 km/h); typical economical cruise, 243 kts (451 km/h) at 16,000 ft (4 877 m) at mean weight of 83,000 lb (37 650 kg); range with max payload, 1,650 naut mls (3 058 km); range with max fuel, 2,320 naut mls (4 300 km).

Accommodation: Flight crew of three or four.

Status: Prototype (military XC-112) first flown 15 February 1946; first production DC-6 flown June 1946; DC-6A first flown 29 September 1949; DC-6B first flown 2 February 1951. DC-7 first flown 18 May 1953; DC-7B first flown 25 April 1955; DC-7C first flown 20 December 1955. Production completed (DC-6) February 1959 (DC-7) December 1958.

Sales: Total of 1,042 DC-6/7 variants built, including 174 DC-6, 73 DC-6A, 288 DC-6B, 168 military, 106 DC-7, 112 DC-7B and 121 DC-7C.

Notes: DC-6 and DC-7, in their successive sub-variants, were progressive extrapolations of the DC-4, with same configuration but various fuselage lengths. About 75 DC-6s were still flying as freighters at the beginning of 1991 (as well as a few DC-4s), but scarcely any DC-7s. *Photo:* DC-6.

HANDLEY PAGE HERALD

Country of Origin: United Kingdom.

Power Plant: Two 2,150 shp (1 603 kW) Rolls-Royce Dart 527 turboprops.

Dimensions: Span, 94 ft 9 in (28,88 m); length, 75 ft 6 in (23,01 m); height, 24 ft 1 in (7,34 m); wing area, 886 sq ft (82,3 m²).

Weights: Operating weight empty, 25,800 lb (11 700 kg); max payload, 11,242 lb (5 100 kg); max zero fuel, 37,500 lb (17 010 kg); max take-off, 43,000 lb (19 505 kg); max landing, 39,500 lb (17 917 kg).

Performance: Max cruise, 274 mph (441 km/h) at 15,000 ft (4 572 m); best economy cruise, 265 mph (426 km/h) at 23,000 ft (7 010 m); range with max payload, 280 naut mls (450 km); range with max fuel, 870 naut mls (1 400 km).

Accommodation: Flight crew of two.

Status: Piston-engined Herald prototypes flown on 25 August 1955 and 3 August 1956; prototypes with Dart engines flown 11 March and 17 December 1958. First production Srs 100 flown 30 October 1959. Prototype Srs 200 flown 8 April 1961; first production Srs 200 flown 13 December 1961. Production completed August 1968.

Sales: Total of 50 built including 36 Srs 200.

Notes: The Herald was one of several small transports developed in the late 'fifties as DC-3 replacements. It competed directly with the Avro 748 and Fokker F27, but had sold less well than either up to the time the Handley Page company ceased trading. Some 14 Heralds were operating in 1990, most of them in the UK for overnight package delivery and *ad hoc* cargo charters. Eight were in the fleet of Channel Express.

ILYUSHIN IL-76

Country of Origin: Soviet Union.
Power Plant: Four 26,455 lb st (12 000 kgp) Soloviev D-30KP-1 turbofans.
Dimensions: Span, 165 ft 8 in (50,50 m); length, 152 ft 10½ in (46,59 m); height, 48 ft 5 in (14,76 m); wing area, 3,229.2 sq ft (300 m²).
Weights (Il-76TD): Max payload, 105,820 lb (48 000 kg); max take-off, 418,875 lb (190 000 kg).
Performance: Max level speed, 459 kts (850 km/h); typical cruise, 405–432 kts (750–800 km/h); range with max payload, 2,700 naut mls (5 000 km); max range, 3,617 naut mls (6 700 km).
Accommodation: Normal flight crew of five (two pilots, flight engineer, navigator, radio operator) plus two freight handlers. Pressurized main cabin, with freight handling equipment.
Status: Prototype first flown 25 March 1971. Service use by Aeroflot began 1975.
Sales: About 200 Il-76T and Il-76TD in service with Aeroflot by end of 1990. Exports to Iraqi Airways, Cubana, Jamahiriya of Libya, Syrianair and Bakhtar Afghan Airlines, totalling more than 75 (for military as well as civil use).
Notes: Development of this long-range freighter was put in hand in the late 'sixties to provide a replacement for the turboprop An-12. The Il-76 has military as well as commercial applications, but those flown by Aeroflot are used primarily to carry heavy supplies associated with engineering and construction activities in the more remote areas of the Soviet Union. Early production aircraft were designated Il-76T; the Il-76TD has improved D-30KP-1 engines, more fuel and higher operating weights. Il-76M military version has a tail turret. Five Il-76TDs are operated by joint Soviet/Swiss cargo airline Metro Cargo for pan-European charter flights.

LOCKHEED ELECTRA

Country of Origin: USA.

Power Plant: Four 3,750 ehp (2 800 kW) Allison 501-D13 turboprops.

Dimensions: Span, 99 ft 0 in (30,18 m); length, 104 ft 6 in (31,81 m); height, 32 ft 10 in (10,0 m); wing area, 1,300 sq ft (120,8 m²).

Weights: Empty equipped, 61,500 lb (27 895 kg); max payload, 26,500 lb (12 020 kg); max fuel, 37,500 lb (17 010 kg); max zero fuel, 86,000 lb (39 010 kg); max take-off, 116,000 lb (52 664 kg); max landing, 95,650 lb (43 387 kg).

Performance: Max cruise, 352 kts (652 km/h) at 22,000 ft (6 700 m); best economy cruise, 325 kts (602 km/h); range with max payload, 1,910 naut mls (3 540 km); range with max fuel, 2,180 naut mls (4 023 km).

Accommodation: Flight crew of two or three.

Status: First of four development aircraft flown 6 December 1957, first production aircraft flown 19 May 1958. Certification 22 August 1958. Re-certification of modified aircraft 5 January 1961. Production completed.

Sales: Total production 170 including 55 L-188C version. About 70 in service in 1991.

Notes: Electra was first airliner of US design and production with turbine power to enter commercial service. Basic variant was L-188A; L-188C had extra fuel and was certificated for higher weights. About 65 Electras remain in service, the majority of these having been converted for use as freighters, with large loading doors in the rear fuselage side and strengthened cabin flooring incorporating roller conveyors to facilitate the handling of pallets and containers.

LOCKHEED L-100 HERCULES

Country of Origin: USA.

Power Plant: Four 4,680 ehp (3 490 kW) Allison 501-D22A turbo-props.

Dimensions (-30): Span, 132 ft 7 in (40,41 m); length, 112 ft 9 in (34,37 m); height, 38 ft 3 in (11,66 m); wing area, 1,745 sq ft (162,12 m²).

Weights (-30): Operating weight empty, 77,680 lb (35 235 kg); max payload, 51,110 lb (23 183 kg); max fuel weight, 64,856 lb (29 418 kg); max take-off, 155,000 lb (70 308 kg); max landing, 135,000 lb (61 236 kg).

Performance: Max cruise, 308 kts (571 km/h) at 20,000 ft (6 100 m); range with max payload (-20), 2,100 naut mls (3 889 km); (-30), 1,363 naut mls (2 526 km); range with max fuel (zero payload) (-20), 4,250 naut mls (7 871 km), (-30), 4,980 naut mls (9 227 km).

Accommodation: Flight crew of three or four.

Status: Lockheed Model 382-44K-20 civil Hercules first flown 21 April 1964 and certificated 16 February 1965. L-100:20 first flown 19 April 1968, certificated 4 October 1968, L-100-30 first flown 14 August 1970, certificated 7 October 1970.

Sales: More than 110 L-100 commercial Hercules sold, of which some 70 operating in 1991.

Notes: The L-100 designation applies to commercial models of the C-130 Hercules, although a few early examples were known by the Lockheed Model 382B designation. The early L-100s were dimensionally similar to the C-130, but the L-100-20 has the fuselage stretched by 8 ft 4 in (2,54 m) and the L-100-30 is longer by another 20 ft (6,1 m). Lockheed projected in 1990 the L-100F dedicated freighter with side-loading door forward of the wing, uprated engines, modernized cockpit and avionics, etc. *Photo:* L-100-30.

SHORT BELFAST

Country of Origin: United Kingdom.

Power Plant: Four 5,730 shp (4 276 kW) Rolls-Royce Tyne RTy 12 turboprops.

Dimensions: Span, 158 ft 10 in (48,41 m); length, 136 ft 5 in (41,58 m); height, 47 ft 0 in (14,33 m); wing area, 2,466 sq ft (229,09 m²).

Weights: Operating weight empty, 130,000 lb (58 597 kg); max payload, 75,000 lb (34 000 kg); fuel load, 82,400 lb (37 376 kg); max zero fuel, 205,000 lb (92 986 kg); max take-off, 230,000 lb (104 325 kg), max landing, 215,000 lb (97 520 kg).

Performance: Max cruise, 306 kts (566 km/h) at 24,000 ft (7 300 m); typical cruise, 275 kts (510 km/h); range with max payload, about 850 naut mls (1 575 km); range with 22,000-lb (10 000-kg) payload, 3,350 naut mls (6 200 km).

Accommodation: Flight crew of three or four. All-freight payload.

Status: First of 10 Belfast C Mk 1s for RAF flown 5 January 1964; deliveries began 20 January 1966. Certificated 6 March 1980.

Sales: Total of 10 aircraft built for RAF. Five acquired ex-RAF for civil conversion in 1977, of which three operated by TAC Heavylift (now Heavylift) with two in reserve.

Notes: The massive Belfast was developed to a specific RAF requirement for a long-range strategic freighter but was withdrawn from service after 10 years. For commercial operation by Heavylift (a subsidiary of the Trafalgar House group), Marshall of Cambridge made a number of modifications to bring systems and equipment into line with contemporary civil standards. Of five aircraft available for conversion, three have been in regular service since 1980.

VICKERS VANGUARD

Country of Origin: United Kingdom.
Power Plant: Four 5,545 eshp (4 135 kW) Rolls-Royce Tyne R Ty.11 Mk 512 turboprops.
Dimensions: Span, 118 ft 7 in (36,15 m); length, 122 ft 10½ in (37,45 m); height, 34 ft 11 in (10,64 m); wing area, 1,529 sq ft (142,0 m²).
Weights: Empty equipped, 82,500 lb (37 422 kg); max payload, 37,000 lb (16 783 kg); max fuel load, 41,130 lb (18 656 kg); max zero fuel, 122,500 lb (55 564 kg); max take-off, 146,500 lb (66 448 kg); max landing, 130,500 lb (61 238 kg).
Performance: High speed cruise, 369 kts (684 km/h) at 20,000 ft (6 100 m); long-range cruise, 365 kts (676 km/h) at 25,000 ft (7 620 m); range with max payload, 1,590 naut mls (2 945 km); range with max fuel and 20,000-lb (9 080-kg) payload, 2,693 naut mls (4 990 km).
Accommodation: Flight crew of two.
Status: Prototype (V-950) flown 20 January 1959; first production V.951 flown 22 April 1959; certificated 2 December 1960. First V.952 flown 21 May 1960. First V.953 flown 1 May 1961. First Merchantman flown 10 October 1969.
Sales: One prototype; six V.951, 23 V.952 and 14 V.953.
Notes: The Vanguard was evolved as an enlarged-capacity successor for the Viscount, but it was overtaken by the first of the short-haul pure jet transports. Twelve of BEA's Vanguards were later converted to V.953C Merchantman standard with cargo loading door in forward fuselage side and cargo handling facilities. In 1990, Air Bridge Carriers and DHL Air operated six and three V.953Cs respectively. *Photo:* V.953C Merchantman.

INDEX

A300, Airbus, 17
A310, Airbus, 19
A320, Airbus, 21
A321, Airbus, 23
A330, Airbus, 25
A340, Airbus, 27
Aero Spacelines Guppy 201, 175
Aérospatiale/Alenia ATR 42, 11
Aérospatiale/Alenia ATR 72, 13
Aérospatiale/BAe Concorde, 15
Aérospatiale Caravelle, 7
Aérospatiale Frégate, 9
Airbus A300, 17
Airbus A310, 19
Airbus A320, 21
Airbus A321, 23
Airbus A330, 25
Airbus A340, 27
Airliner, Beechcraft 1900, 35
Airtech CN-235, 29
Allison Flagship, 77
An-12, 176
An-14M, 33
An-22, 176
An-24, 31
An-26, 31
An-28, 33
An-30, 31
An-32, 31
An-72, 178
An-74, 178
An-124, 179
Antheus, An-22, 176
Antonov An-12, 176
Antonov An-14M, 33
Antonov An-22, 176
Antonov An-24, 31
Antonov An-26, 31
Antonov An-28, 33
Antonov An-30, 31
Antonov An-32, 31
Antonov An-72, 178
Antonov An-74, 178
Antonov An-124, 179
ATP, British Aerospace, 65
ATR 42, Aérospatiale/Alenia, 11
ATR 72, Aérospatiale/Alenia, 13
Aviocar, CASA C-212, 75
Avro 748, 63

BAC One-Eleven, 71
BAe ATP, 65
BAe 146 Srs 100/200, 59
BAe 146 Srs 300, 61
BAe RJ70, 59
BAe RJ80, 59
Bandeirante, Embraer, 95
Beechcraft 1900 Airliner, 35
Belfast, Short, 188
Boeing 707-320, 37
Boeing 727, 39
Boeing 737-200, 41
Boeing 737-300, 43
Boeing 747-100/200, 47
Boeing 747-300/400, 49
Boeing 757, 51
Boeing 767-200, 53
Boeing 767-300, 55
Boeing 777, 57
Brasilia, Embraer EMB-120, 97
British Aerospace ATP, 65
British Aerospace (BAC) One-
   Eleven, 71
British Aerospace BAe 146 Srs
   100/200, 59
British Aerospace BAe 146 Srs
   300, 61
British Aerospace Concorde, 15
British Aerospace HS.748, 63
British Aerospace Jetstream 31,
   67
British Aerospace Jetstream 41,
   69
British Aerospace RJ70, RJ80, 59

C-46, Curtiss Commando, 182
C-47, Douglas Skytrain, 93
C-130, Lockheed Hercules, 187
C-212, CASA Aviocar, 75
Canadair CL-44, 180
Canadair CL-601, 73
Canadair RJ, 73
Caravan 1, Cessna, 181
Caravelle, Aérospatiale, 7
Cargomaster, Cessna 208, 181
CASA C-212 Aviocar, 75
CASA-Nurtanio CN-235, 29
CBA-123, Embraer/FMA, 101
Cessna 208 Caravan 1, 181

CL-44, Canadair, 180
CL-601, Canadair RJ, 73
CN-235, Airtech, 29
CNIAR One-Eleven 2000, 71
Commando, Curtiss C-46, 182
Concorde, Aérospatiale/BAe, 15
Convair 580, 77
Convair 600, 77
Convair 640, 77
Curtiss C-46, 182

Dakota, Douglas, 93
Dash 7, de Havilland Canada, 83
Dash 8-100, DHC, 85
Dash 8-300, DHC, 87
Dassault-Breguet Mercure, 79
DC-3, Douglas, 93
DC-6, Douglas, 183
DC-7, Douglas, 183
DC-8, Douglas, 135
DC-9 Srs 10/20/30, McDonnell
  Douglas, 137
DC-9 Srs 40/50, McDonnell
  Douglas, 139
DC-9 Super 80, McDonnell
  Douglas, 141
DC-10, McDonnell Douglas, 147
Dee Howard One-Eleven 2400, 71
De Havilland Canada Dash 7, 83
De Havilland Canada Dash 8-100,
  85
De Havilland Canada Dash 8-300,
  87
De Havilland Canada Twin Otter,
  81
Deutsche Aerospace 228, 89
Deutsche Aerospace 328, 91
DHC-6 Twin Otter, 81
DHC-7, de Havilland Canada, 83
DHC-8 Srs 100, 85
DHC-8 Srs 300, 87
Dornier 228, 89
Dornier 328, 91
Douglas DC-3, 93
Douglas DC-6, 183
Douglas DC-7, 183
Douglas DC-8, 135
Douglas DC-9, Srs 10/20/30, 137
Douglas DC-9 Srs 40/50, 139
Douglas DC-9 Super 80, 141
Douglas DC-10, 147

Electra, Lockheed, 186
EMB-110 Bandeirante, Embraer,
  95
EMB-120 Brasilia, Embraer, 97
EMB-145, Embraer, 99
Embraer Bandeirante, 95
Embraer EMB-120 Brasilia, 97
Embraer EMB-145, 99
Embraer/FMA Vector, 101

F-27, Fairchild, 103
F27, Fokker Friendship, 107
F28, Fokker Fellowship, 111
Fairchild F-27, 103
Fairchild FH-227, 103
Fairchild Metro III, 105
Fellowship, Fokker F28, 111
FH-227, Fairchild, 103
Fokker F27 Friendship, 107
Fokker F28 Fellowship, 111
Fokker 50, 109
Fokker 100, 113
Fokker 130, 113
Frégate, Aérospatiale, 9
Friendship, Fokker F27, 107

G-1C, Gulfstream American, 115
Grand Caravan, Cessna 208, 181
Grumman Gulfstream 1, 115
Gulfstream 1, Grumman, 115
Gulfstream Aerospace G1-C, 115
Guppy 201, Aero Spacelines, 175

Handley Page Herald, 184
Hawker Siddeley HS.748, 63
Herald, Handley Page, 184
Hercules, Lockheed L-100, 187
HS.748, British Aerospace, 63

Il-18, Ilyushin, 117
Il-62, Ilyushin, 119
Il-76, Ilyushin, 185
Il-86, Ilyushin, 121
Il-96, Ilyushin, 123
Il-114, Ilyushin, 125
Ilyushin Il-18, 117
Ilyushin Il-62, 119
Ilyushin Il-76, 185
Ilyushin Il-86, 121
Ilyushin Il-96, 123
Ilyushin Il-114, 125

Jet stream 31, BAe, 67
`Jetstream 41, BAe, 69
Jet Trader, Douglas DC-8, 135

L-100, Lockheed Hercules, 187
L-410, Let, 127
L-610, Let, 129
L-1011-100/200 Lockheed
    TriStar, 131
L-1011-500 Lockheed TriStar,
    133
Let L-410, 127
Let L-610, 129
Lockheed Electra, 186
Lockheed L-100 Hercules, 187
Lockheed L-1011-100/200
    TriStar, 131
Lockheed L-1011-500 TriStar,
    133

McDonnell Douglas DC-8, 135
McDonnell Douglas DC-9 Srs 10/
    20/30, 137
McDonnell Douglas DC-9 Srs 40/
    50, 139
McDonnell Douglas DC-9 Super
    80, 141
McDonnell Douglas MD-80/83,
    141
McDonnell Douglas MD-87, 143
McDonnell Douglas MD-90, 145
McDonnell Douglas DC-10, 147
McDonnell Douglas MD-11, 149
McDonnell Douglas MD-12, 149
Max Holste MH 250, 9
Max Holste MH 260, 9
MD-11, 149
MD-12, 149
MD-80, 141
MD-81, 141
MD-82, 141
MD-83, 141
MD-87, 143
MD-88, 141
MD-90, 145
Mercure, Dassault-Breguet, 79
Merchantman, Vickers, 189
Metro III, Fairchild, 105
Mohawk 298, Aérospatiale/Nord
    262, 9

NAMC YS-11, 151
Nord 262, 9
Nurtanio CN-235, 29

One-Eleven, BAe (BAC), 71

Regional Jet, Canadair, 73
RJ, Canadair, 73

Saab 340, 153
Saab 2000, 155
SD3-30, Shorts, 157
SF-340, Saab, 153
Sherpa, Shorts 330, 157
Shorts 330, 157
Shorts 360, 159
Short Belfast, 188
Sud Caravelle, 7
Super 580, Convair, 77
Super Cargomaster, Cessna 208,
    181
Swearingen Metro III, 105

TriStar 100/200, Lockheed, 131
TriStar 500, Lockheed, 133
Tu-134, Tupolev, 161
Tu-154, Tupolev, 163
Tu-155, Tupolev, 163
Tu-156, Tupolev, 163
Tu-204, Tupolev, 165
Tupolev Tu-134, 161
Tupolev Tu-154, 163
Tupolev Tu-155, 163
Tupolev Tu-156, 163
Tupolev, Tu-204, 165
Twin Otter, DHC, 81

Vanguard, Vickers, 189
Vector, Embraer/FMA, 101
Vickers Vanguard, 189
Vickers Viscount, 167
Viscount, Vickers, 167

Xian Y7, 169

Y7, Xian, 169
Yak-40, 171
Yak-42, 173
Yakovlev Yak-40, 171
Yakovlev Yak-42, 173
YS-11, NAMC, 151